The Random House Book of
Birds

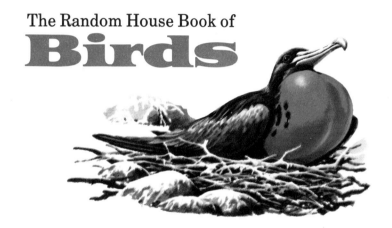

The Random House Book of

Birds

Elizabeth S. Austin

and

Oliver L. Austin, Jr.

Illustrated by Richard E. Amundsen

RANDOM HOUSE · NEW YORK

We are most grateful to Dr. Mary Heimerdinger Clench, Associate Curator of Birds at the Carnegie Museum of Pittsburgh, Pennsylvania, for her careful reading of the manuscript and her helpful suggestions. Dr. Pierce Brodkorb of the faculty of the University of Florida and Dr. E. G. Franz Sauer, Director of the Natural History Museum, University of Bonn, Germany, have been most generous with information and we thank them sincerely. We also appreciate the cooperation of the staff of the University of Florida Research Library.

Photograph credits: Interior—Sport Fisheries & Wildlife (Rex Gary Schmidt): 1; Father Mulligan, St. Louis University: 110.

The Random House Book of
Birds

Introduction

Birds evolved more than 150 million years ago from a reptilelike ancestor. Today they still wear reptilian scales on their legs and they start life as most reptiles do by hatching out of eggs. In other ways birds are more like mammals. They are warm-blooded, can maintain their own body temperature, and remain active in cold weather when reptiles must hibernate.

Flight is an important part of the life of most birds. Flying birds have the lightest skeletons of any vertebrate animals. Their larger bones are hollow, and they have inflatable sacs like small balloons within their bodies connected to their lungs. Some travel great distances. The Arctic tern travels 25,000 miles each year back and forth between its northern nesting ground and its southern wintering ground. When they migrate, birds navigate by watching the sun and stars. Birds that fly in dark caves, like the oilbird of South America, find their way by listening to the echoes of their own voices.

Birds share their ability to fly and to migrate with other vertebrate animals. Bats are mammals that fly, and eels are fishes that migrate 5,000 miles or more to and from their breeding grounds.

Birds have just one attribute that sets them apart from all other living creatures. They have feathers, which no other animal has. Many birds have another attribute that sets them apart from all other creatures but man. They can sing melodies.

Today we know of at least 8,650 species or different kinds of birds. These are divided into about 155 family groups according to their resemblances to one another. Some families are very small. The limpkin family has only one species and the turkey family two species. The largest bird family is the sparrow family with 375 species.

In the spring most birds go courting. Part of the courtship is establishing a home place in which to raise a family. Some species build nests, some use holes in trees or bird boxes, some dig burrows, and some just make a saucer-shaped hollow in the ground. In some species the female lays only one egg, in others a clutch of 3 or 4, and in some such as the guinea fowl a clutch of as many as 20 eggs.

To hatch, eggs must be kept at an even warm temperature. Most birds do this by sitting over their eggs. But a few birds do it differently. The Australian mallee fowl of the mound builder family buries its eggs in its mound of vegetable matter which becomes warm as it rots. When the germ of life, the embryo, within the egg has developed into a chick, this little bird pecks and kicks at its shell until it breaks its way out. After a bird has hatched it is usually guarded and fed by one or both parents, until it can care for itself.

In the spring of 1804 John James Audubon wanted to be able to recognize the phoebes near his home in Pennsylvania. He tied a bit of silver wire to a leg of each bird. The following year when the phoebes returned to use their old nests, he proved they were the same phoebes because each bird had his silver wire on its leg.

This is the first record of bird banding in America. American bands today are flexible aluminum strips that can be clamped loosely around a bird's leg. A number and the words "Fish & Wildlife Service Wash. D. C." are etched on each band. In North America about 2,000 people with banding permits band $2\frac{1}{2}$ million birds each year. Putting a numbered band on a bird's leg and recording the place where it was done is like giving the bird a name and address.

At the Bird Banding Laboratory, Department of the Interior, Washington, D. C., a record is kept of every bird wearing an American band, telling where and when it was put on and, if possible, the age and sex of the bird. When a band is found and reported, the Banding Laboratory sends all the information about the bird that wore the band to both the finder and the original bander. At least 70,000 bands are found each year and their numbers reported to the Bird Banding Laboratory. Hunters report the bands on game birds they kill, beachcombers pick up dead banded birds, motorists stop to examine road kills, and many a band is taken from a bird killed by a cat. Children, who are often more observant than adults, find and send in many bands.

Banding has let us trace migration routes accurately. Golden plovers fly from Alaska as far as New Zealand and Australia with stopovers on Pacific islands. Chimney swifts disappear from the United States in the fall. We discovered their winter home when Indians in Peru brought bands they had found to a trader.

From bird banding we have learned the ages of birds in the wild. A sooty tern banded as a nestling on the Dry Tortugas Islands in Florida was recaptured and released in good health 30 years later. A cardinal has lived 13 years and a brown thrasher 12 years.

Banding is done on all continents and in many countries. In England and Europe it is called bird ringing and is run by a private trust. Birds do not pay any attention to international boundaries. Turnstones banded by the Japanese have been picked up in Alaska. More than 400 birds banded in America have been recovered in eastern Russia. Many warblers and flycatchers that breed in North America winter in South America.

Much of what this book tells of bird behavior, travels, and populations has been learned through bird banding. It is a most important tool to the science of bird study and through it more has been learned about birds in the last 50 years than during all the centuries before. Among the many scientists to whom we are grateful for information used in this book are the bird banders of the world, professional and amateur.

In our illustrations we have indicated sex by the symbols all scientists use. They are the signs astronomers use for the planets. The mirror of Venus ♀ indicates female and the arrow of Mars ♂ male. When no sign is used, the male and female birds are similar.

Banding a Canada goose at a wildlife refuge in Maryland. The man at the left is holding the band in order to read the number on it.

1

Albatrosses

Laysan Albatross

Black-footed Albatross

The world's largest sea birds are the 13 different albatrosses. Albatrosses spend most of their lives soaring with the winds over the ocean seas. They glide low over the waves when searching for fish and climb higher into the air when following ships. If a gale is blowing, they sail on it with their wings almost motionless. If the wind slackens they flap their wings. When there is no wind they have trouble flying and must rest on the water until it blows again. Then they spread their wings, flap them hard, and run over the surface of the water until they are once more airborne.

Over the seas of the Southern Hemisphere 10 species of albatrosses roam from the Antarctic northward to those parts of the oceans near the equator called the "doldrums" where winds rarely blow. The birds cannot cross the doldrums, but on the other side of them in the North Pacific live 3 other kinds of albatrosses. These are the only albatrosses seen in United States waters. The BLACK-FOOTED ALBATROSS and the LAYSAN ALBATROSS breed in the Hawaiian Islands. They cruise to Alaska and off the coast of California. The SHORT-TAILED ALBA-

TROSS nests on islands south of Japan and cruises from the China Sea to the coast of North America.

The WANDERING ALBATROSS is the largest one. It lives south of the doldrums in the Pacific, Atlantic, and Indian Oceans. Adult males are 4 feet long from bill-tip to tail-tip and weigh only about 25 pounds, but their narrow wings when spread span 10 to 11½ feet. Even the smallest albatross, the black-footed, has a wing span of 7 or 8 feet.

Scientists call the albatrosses and their relatives, the petrels and shearwaters, the *Tubinares*, meaning the tube-noses, because their nostrils open into horny tubes that grow out of their bills, one on either side of each albatross's stout, hook-ended, horn-plated beak.

Albatrosses nest on remote ocean islands. From October to December, the warm season of the year in the seas south of the equator, adult albatrosses (7 or more years old) return to their nesting grounds,

2

each species to its own special island. Male birds court the females by posing and dancing. When a female joins a male in his dance, she has accepted him as her mate.

Wandering albatross pairs nest every other year, the smaller species every year. They lay their single white egg in a hollow scoop in the ground or a mud nest lined with grass and feathers, depending on the species. The egg is in-cubated by both parents, one sitting while the other feeds at sea. Eggs of the smaller albatrosses hatch in 65 days. The wandering albatross egg takes 80 days to hatch. It is another 3 to 6 months before the young albatrosses can fly. Until they do the parents feed them half-digested squid and other surface sea-foods, which the adults gush out of their throats into the open mouths of the chicks.

Anhingas

These fresh-water birds live in Africa and from southern Asia to Australia. The American ANHINGA lives from Oklahoma, Tennessee, and North Carolina southward to Argentina. Anhingas are among the few water birds whose feathers are not waterproof. After diving and swimming under water to spear a fish with its long, thin, pointed bill, an anhinga must dry its feathers. To do this it perches on a branch and spreads its wings in the sun.

In the water anhingas often swim with only their slender heads and snakelike necks above the surface. From this habit they are called "snake birds" or "darters."

Anhingas build bulky nests of sticks in trees from 3 to 30 feet up. They choose trees near or over the water. Both parents incubate their 3 to 6 bluish-white eggs and feed and care for the young. The young are naked when hatched, but soon grow a coat of white down, and in 3 weeks their tail and wing feathers start to sprout.

Anis

See Cuckoos

Auks

This is a family of 22 living species of northern sea birds. They breed at the edges of the Arctic Ocean. Most of them migrate southward to avoid the ice in winter. Those that breed where the sea does not freeze may remain near their breeding grounds the year around. Two species of auk, the BLACK GUILLEMOT and the DOVEKIE, nest within the Arctic Circle and migrate south to New England waters. The WHISKERED AUKLET breeds on Alaska's Aleutian Islands and stays there all year.

Auks are to the far north what penguins are to the Antarctic. Like penguins, they stand erect and sway as they walk. They are chunky birds with large heads and short necks, legs, and tails. Their small, strong wings have short flight feathers near the body and long ones on the wing tips. For underwater swimming, auks use their wings like oars and their 3-toed webbed feet as rudders for steering. They also steer with their feet when they fly, and they fly well with powerful wing beats.

Auks fish by diving into the water from the surface. They eat fish, shellfish, sea worms, and seaweed.

Auks change their plumage twice each year. Through the white winter of the north they wear more white feathers. The black guillemot in summer has a white wing patch. In winter it is an almost white bird. In spring, many auks grow courting plumes or crests or colored bills or special markings on the throat and head.

Except for the puffins, auks are especially noisy during the breeding season. They grunt, moan, yelp, and hiss. Perhaps to make up for their silence, puffins grow huge bright horny bill covers, with which they gesture, do their courting and threaten their enemies. Mated puffins rub their gaudy beaks together. Puffins nest at the end of a 2- to 4-foot burrow they dig with their beaks and claws. When feeding a chick a parent COMMON PUFFIN can carry as many as 30 small fish in its bill at once. The chick remains in the burrow 40 days and then crawls to the sea before it can fly.

Two of the largest auks, 16 to 19 inches long, are the COMMON MURRE and the RAZOR-BILLED AUK. They come ashore only in spring to breed and nest in close-packed colonies on cliff sides.

Auks always enjoy each other's company, so courtship in the auk family begins in a crowd out on the ocean. The

Great Auk with egg (extinct)

Black Guillemot (winter plumage)

birds dip and bow and dive in a water ballet. When mated, they fly to high cliffs that face the sea. Each pair incubates its single egg and raises its chick crowded wing to wing with other pairs on narrow ledges. The eggs are shaped like a top. If an egg is touched, it rolls around the pointed end instead of rolling off the ledge. Two weeks after the chicks hatch, and when they are only half the size of adults, they flutter down to the water where their parents join them for a first fishing trip.

The black guillemot, the only auk that lays 2 eggs, and the little 7-inch dovekie also nest on cliffs but hide their eggs and their chicks under rocks. These chicks, protected from raiding gulls and arctic foxes, remain in the nest hole for 6 to 8 weeks until they can fly to the sea. Male and female dovekies carry tiny shellfish in cheek pouches when feeding their single chick. After the breeding season the pouches shrink away. Dovekies are a delicacy for the Eskimos of Greenland who call them "sea-kings."

The twenty-third member of the auk family lives only in history and legend. The GREAT AUK, a 30-inch-long flightless species, once bred on North Atlantic islands near the Arctic Circle. It was a powerful swimmer. In winter it swam as far south as the coast of Florida in America and Gibraltar in Europe. On its breeding grounds it could not defend itself or escape into the air. It was easily herded into pens and captured or shot for meat, oil, and feathers. The last 2 great auks were killed on an islet off Iceland on June 3, 1844.

Common Murre

Whiskered Auklet

Common Puffin

Dovekie

Avocets

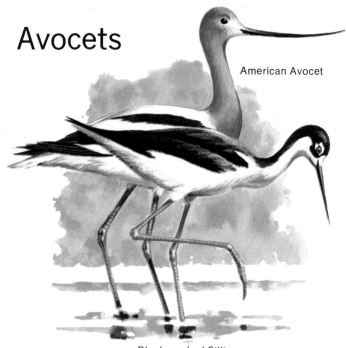

American Avocet

Black-necked Stilt

The AMERICAN AVOCET swings its up-curved bill through the water like a sickle in search of shrimps and water insects. No other birds have up-curved bills. Avocets usually lay 4 eggs in a shallow scrape near water. If the water rises they push grass and shells under the eggs to keep them dry.

Some of the 7 members of the avocet family have straight bills. These straight-billed birds are called stilts, for that is what their very long legs look like. The BLACK-NECKED STILT probes deeply into mud with its straight bill for its food. It lives from the southern and western United States to northern South America.

Birds of Paradise

This is a family of 40 kinds of perching birds known for the brilliantly colored and fantastically shaped plumage of the males. Thirty-six species are native to New Guinea and neighboring islands. Four are found in northeastern Australia.

Nobody knows what year the first bird of paradise feathers were brought from the far Pacific to Europe. Perhaps they came in the late 1400's. Magellan brought 2 skins to Spain in 1522. They were a gift from the ruler of Batjan, one of the Molucca Islands. The early description of them fits WALLACE'S STANDARD-WINGED BIRD OF PARADISE, the westernmost bird of paradise and the only one native to Batjan. This bird has 4 white plumes or "standards" that grow from its back, 2 from each shoulder. He can raise these plumes in the air or lower them at will. When courting, Wallace's standard-wing fluffs out his beautiful green collar while posing and posturing. The female is a dull brown bird, as most female birds of paradise are.

Birds of paradise are distantly related to crows, and the largest ones are about the size of a common crow. They are all as noisy as crows. The call of the GREATER BIRD OF PARADISE, a loud shrill

"wowk-wowk-wowk-wak-wak-wak," can be heard all over the forests of New Guinea and the Aru Islands just south of western New Guinea. Male greater birds of paradise court in groups of 12 to 20 in what the natives call dancing parties. They gather in a tall tree with many branches and few leaves. They perch, bend their heads down, stretch their necks out, hump their backs, spread their wings, and raise their plumes. They shiver and shake as they compete for the attention of the plain, reddish females.

All birds of paradise that scientists have watched breed in much the same way. The females build large nests, in which they lay 2 brown-streaked orange eggs. Without any help from the male birds, who may have several mates, each female incubates her eggs and feeds and cares for her young.

Six species are called the manucodes. These are glossy birds with no plumes. The BLACK MANUCODE takes only one mate. He brings material to her when she builds the nest and helps her care for their young.

Male MCGREGOR'S BIRDS OF PARADISE and WATTLED BIRDS OF PARADISE, both

King of Saxony
Bird of Paradise
♂

King Bird of Paradise
♂

♂

Red-plumed Bird of Paradise

Prince Rudolph's
♂
Blue Bird of Paradise

♂

Magnificent Bird of Paradise

with yellow wattles in front of their eyes, behave like the manucodes. McGregor's bird of paradise lives on mountain tops 10,000 feet above sea level in New Guinea. One species, the KING BIRD OF PARADISE, the smallest member of the family, nests in a hole in a tree.

The plumes of birds of paradise were once used for ladies' hats, capes, and fans. The species that brought the highest prices came close to extinction. Among these were the LESSER BIRD OF PARADISE, who displays a shower of fine blue plumes and two longer wiry black ones while hanging upside down from a branch; the EMPEROR OF GERMANY'S BIRD OF PARADISE, who grows a fountain of golden and cream plumes above his emerald head in the same topsy-turvy fashion; and the greater bird of paradise. Strict laws passed in 1924 saved these birds from the traders and the native hunters.

Bitterns

See Herons

Blackbirds

Baltimore Oriole ♂

Bullock's Oriole ♂

The scientific name of this American family of 6- to 21-inch land birds is the Icteridae from the Latin word for yellow. Many of the family's 94 species are as much yellow or orange birds as they are black birds. Icterids are the only North American songbirds without bristles around their bills. This sets them apart from the tanagers and sparrows.

Icterids range all over the Western Hemisphere except the far north where trees no longer grow and South America's icy southern tip. Seventy-four species are native to South and Central America. Most of these live in the tropics. Among the 20 species native to North America are some of our most familiar birds: BALTIMORE and BULLOCK'S ORIOLES, EASTERN and WESTERN MEADOWLARKS, BOBOLINKS, COMMON and BOAT-TAILED GRACKLES, BROWN-HEADED COWBIRDS, also RED-WINGED, YELLOW-HEADED, and RUSTY BLACKBIRDS.

Many icterids live in forests, but meadowlarks and bobolinks prefer open fields. Red-winged and yellow-headed blackbirds live in marshes. SCOTT'S ORIOLE is at home only on the edge of deserts in southwestern United States. Here it hangs its cup-shaped nest of woven yucca fibers 4 to 10 feet up in a yucca or cactus tree. It raises two families of three chicks each during each summer.

All icterids eat insects and seeds. The orioles add fruit to this diet and sometimes vegetables. The grackles eat everything their relatives do and also small mammals, amphibians, reptiles, birds and other birds' eggs. Common grackles join other icterids in raiding grain fields. With the yellow-headed and red-winged blackbirds, they do much damage to corn crops in the Midwest. On the other hand BREWER'S BLACKBIRD is a help to the

♂

Red-winged Blackbird

farmers of the West because it eats so many crickets, grasshoppers, boll weevils, and alfalfa weevils.

The bobolink was known as the "rice bird" or the "reed bird" in the southeastern United States when rice was grown there. During migration between their northern breeding grounds and their South American winter home thousands of bobolinks used to descend on the rice fields to feast on the ripening grain. The

Western Meadowlark

Bobolink ♂

plantation-owners sent hunters to shoot the birds and then feasted on them. Now bobolinks, like most songbirds, are protected by law.

Brown-headed cowbirds once followed the herds of buffaloes on the plains. Now they follow cattle to eat the insects the cows stir up as they graze.

Male icterids usually wear the bright feathers. The females are mostly dull brown. But male and female common grackles and meadowlarks wear the same dress. Male icterids also do all the singing. The bubbling song of the bobolink, the thin whistle of the brown-headed cowbird, and the fluty tones of the Baltimore orioles all come from the swelling throats of courting male birds in spring. Male icterids never incubate eggs and rarely help in the feeding and care of young birds.

Most blackbirds build strong well-made nests. The orioles are well known for their long hanging nests. Oropendolas,

large tropical orioles, build amazing ones. MONTEZUMA'S OROPENDOLA, a 19-inch-long icterid of Central America, weaves a raindrop-shaped basket with a neck as much as 6 feet long, down which the female climbs to incubate her eggs. These birds live in colonies and as many as a hundred of their stockinglike nests may hang on one tall tree, waving in the breezes. The nests are all built by the females, 2 or 3 of whom share 1 male. North American orioles build much shallower nests.

A few members of the blackbird family, all cowbirds, do not build any nests at all. The cowbird females lay their eggs in the nests of other species among the eggs of the rightful owners. The cowbirds leave the eggs to be incubated and hatched by the hosts, who will raise the chicks with their own nestlings. Often the cowbird chicks push the smaller chicks out of the nest or demand the lion's share of food. BRONZE COWBIRDS usually lay in the nests of their relatives, the orioles, and rarely use other species. The GIANT COWBIRD of Central America rides on

♂

Brown-headed Cowbird

9

the backs of cattle to hunt ticks. It uses the nests of oropendolas and other tropical American icterids, the CACIQUES, who build hanging nests similar to those of oropendolas.

After the breeding season is over, all North American blackbirds except the orioles and meadowlarks gather together in great flocks. They migrate and feed in flocks. At night the flocks gather to-gether to roost. There may be a million or more birds in one grove of trees or wooded swamp. Blackbirds are probably more plentiful than any other family of land birds in the New World.

There are no icterids in Europe, and the "Four and twenty blackbirds baked in a pie" of the nursery rhyme were English thrushes, much like our robin but all black in color.

Bluebirds

See Thrushes

Bobolinks

See Blackbirds

Boobies

See Gannets

Bowerbirds

♂   Queensland Gardener Bowerbird

Male bowerbirds make up for their lack of bright courting plumage by building ornate courting grounds. They pile twigs and grasses to make a platform and put nest-like huts or grass- and twig-walled passages upon it or on cleared ground. The birds decorate these courting grounds with leaves, flowers, berries, shells, fruit, feathers, and other bright objects. To 19th-century explorers in Australia the courting grounds looked like the summer houses then called "bowers."

Male bowerbirds lure females by singing loudly and clearly from a perch near their courting arenas or from the platform itself. In addition to their own calls, some mimic other birds and forest creatures. The females come and stand within the grass shelters to watch the males pose and display themselves. After mating a female goes off to build a cup-shaped nest high in a tree. She lays 2 eggs and incubates them and raises her young without any help from the male. He continues to sing and pose in his courting place.

The 13-inch SATIN BOWERBIRD marks the inside walls of his grassy passage with a colored mixture of charcoal and saliva or fruit pulp. He applies this paint with a bit of shredded bark he holds in his bill. The satin bowerbird prefers to decorate with blue feathers and greenish-yellow flowers. He dislikes red.

The 9½-inch QUEENSLAND GARDENER BOWERBIRD finds 2 sapling trees growing 3 or 4 feet apart and builds a hut-like structure around each. He occupies the same territory each year and keeps adding to the size of the huts. He joins them near the ground so his bower is U-shaped. The Queensland gardener decorates with orchids and mosses. These take root and continue to grow after he strews them on his courting place in the tropical rain forests of Australia.

Buntings

Bunting is an ancient English name for seed-eating birds of the sparrow family whose males have bright patches of solidly colored plumage. Early British settlers gave the name to a number of the New World sparrows that reminded them of the buntings in England. The male PAINTED BUNTING in his dress of vivid red, green and blue is the showiest bird in southeastern North America. The LARK BUNTING of the western plains and prairies is the state bird of Colorado. The INDIGO BUNTING breeds from Canada to the Gulf States and winters in Central America and Cuba, where the bright blue male becomes a dull brown like the female. The SNOW BUNTING breeds in the Arctic and subarctic around the world. It winters south to Pennsylvania, England and southern Siberia.

See also: SPARROWS AND RELATED BIRDS

Painted Bunting
♀

Lark Bunting
♂

Snow Bunting

Canaries

The Canary Islands are the native home of these singing finches, now the commonest cage birds the world around. When CANARY FINCHES were first brought to Europe, they were brown-flecked olive-green birds with yellow-green breasts. Europeans bred them for voice and color and discovered that the birds would mate with closely related European birds, the yellowish SISKIN and EUROPEAN GOLDFINCH. By 1587 they were described as being entirely yellow except for the wing tips.

Caracaras

These strange falcons fly like eagles, walk, run, and eat carrion like vultures, but also take live prey like other falcons. AUDUBON'S CARACARA breeds from southern Florida, Texas, Arizona, and southward through Mexico and Central America. Sometimes called the Mexican Eagle or the Mexican Buzzard, it is the national bird of Mexico. The GUADALUPE CARACARA is extinct, killed by the sheep-raising Guadalupe Islanders because it preyed on new-born lambs.
See also: FALCONS

Cardinals

A glowing shade of red was called cardinal, as the bird now is, before America and its red finch were discovered. The EASTERN CARDINAL lives east of the Great Plains in the United States and in southernmost Canada and parts of Mexico. It is also found on the Gulf of California and the West Indies. It was introduced in 1929 to Hawaii. The cardinal is a bird of many names—redbird, Virginia nightingale, Kentucky cardinal, and cardinal grosbeak. In the subtropics the males sing their song almost all year long. "What-cheer, what-cheer-cheer-cheer," they call in gardens and country hedges in spring.
See also: SPARROWS AND RELATED BIRDS

Canary Finch

Audubon's Caracara

♂ Cardinal

Chickadees

Black-capped Chickadee

Boreal Chickadee

Those members of the titmouse family that wear black caps and bibs and are less than $4\frac{3}{4}$ inches long are known as chickadees, for they all sing "chickadee, dee, dee." The BLACK-CAPPED CHICKADEE nests in Canada and the northern United States and only strays a few miles farther south in winter. The BOREAL CHICKADEE is a year-round resident in Alaska, Canada, and the states along the Canadian border. The CAROLINA CHICKADEE lives all year long in the southeastern United States from southern Illinois and New Jersey to the Gulf of Mexico and central Florida.

See also: TITMICE

Buff Orpington

Longtailed Yokohama   White Plymouth Rock

Chickens

Chickens are domestic birds, tamed in prehistoric times, probably about 6,000 years ago. Their ancestors were the jungle fowl of southeast Asia. Most chickens in America are bred, like the White Leghorn or the Buff Orpington, to provide eggs and meat. A few are bred for their beautiful plumage by poultry fanciers. In other countries chickens are bred for the fighting qualities of the males. Cockfights are considered cruel sport in this country but are legal in many other lands. In Japan the roosters of one kind of fowl, the Longtailed Yokohama, are raised for the length of their beautiful tails which may grow to be 20 feet of trailing feathers. In South America the Araucana, a chicken, is prized for its eggs with blue shells.

See also: DOMESTIC BIRDS; PHEASANTS

Condors

See Vultures

Coots

See Rails

Cormorants

Great Cormorant

These web-footed water birds are at home in large lakes and rivers as well as on the seacoasts of the world. They never go far from land. The smallest is the 19-inch PYGMY CORMORANT of the inland waters of southeastern Europe. The largest is the 40-inch GREAT CORMORANT. A long bird with a long range and a long life, it possibly lives to be 36 or 40 years old.

The FLIGHTLESS CORMORANT of the Galapagos Islands does not fly at all, but the other 29 kinds fly strongly. They occasionally coast on the winds, but otherwise cormorant flight is much like that of geese. With strong, even wing beats, they fly in formation or in groups. Northern cormorants such as the DOUBLE-CRESTED CORMORANT of North America migrate.

Cormorants swim low in the water and feed by diving from the surface to chase fish under water. Most of them stay in water 12 to 25 feet deep, but fishermen have caught many PELAGIC CORMORANTS in nets set 180 feet down in the sea off the coast of California.

After a fish has been caught, a cormorant always swims to the surface of the water with its catch. The bird tosses the fish into the air or twists it about in its beak so the fish can be swallowed head first. When a cormorant has eaten enough it goes to a perch, a buoy, or a rock or tree and spreads its wings to dry. After its meal has been digested the cormorant spits out 1- to 2-inch balls of fish bones, held together in a gluelike mass. Along the seacoasts cormorants eat eels, and fish such as tom cod, sea worms, and shellfish. In lakes they eat fish, frogs and other amphibians.

Cormorants breed in colonies. They put their bulky nests on the ground or in trees. They make their nests of sticks, bark, twigs and grasses woven with seaweed, kelp, and rockweed. Both parents incubate the 2 to 4 eggs. The black-skinned young are born naked and blind. The parents feed them on half-digested food which the chicks sip from the adults' beaks. In 3 weeks the chicks are covered with black down.

Cormorants have been of great benefit to man. Their droppings, called guano, are a valuable fertilizer. The CAPE CORMORANT of South Africa is protected and supplied with nesting platforms because of its valuable guano. Until very recently double-crested cormorants were supplied with roosting racks in Florida so their guano could be collected and used for fertilizer by Florida farmers.

In Japan and China the great cormorant has been used for fishing for hundreds of years. Japanese fishermen still take teams of about a dozen cormorants out in their boats at dusk to fish on rivers. Each bird is on a leather leash with a ring around its neck. The ring stops it from swallowing the fish that it catches. The cormorant returns to its owner when its throat pouch is full, disgorges the fish, and is fed its share.

Cowbirds

See Blackbirds

Cranes

The largest wading bird in the world is the 5-foot-long SARUS CRANE of southern India. It is also one of the best protected birds in the world, because the people of India believe it is bad luck to injure or kill a crane. The sarus cranes are very tame, and mated pairs become household pets, live in the garden, and act as watchdogs, warning the family when strangers approach. The pair in the wild or in a garden remain together for life.

The 50-inch WHOOPING CRANE of America is a victim of man-made changes in its wintering grounds and of illegal shooting. Once as plentiful as any crane in the world, now it is reduced to only a few birds.

The SANDHILL CRANE stands $3\frac{1}{2}$ feet tall. It is found throughout North America west of the Mississippi and also in Florida and Cuba in suitable wet prairies, fields, and marshes. In flat country it can be seen from miles away.

All cranes have straight, strong bills as long as or a little longer than their heads. They have ornamental plumes or areas of bare red skin on their heads. The 3-foot DEMOISELLE CRANE of south-central Eurasia wears white plumes on either side of its head. The 38-inch CROWNED CRANE of Africa wears a bristly golden

Sandhill Crane

Whooping Crane

Demoiselle Crane

whiskbroom for a crown, white earmuffs, and a red patch under its chin.

Cranes do elaborate group dances. Some species dance only during the breeding season and some the year round. The dance starts when two birds strut around each other with half-open wings. They bow to each other, stretch their necks and bills toward the sky, and then like partners in a ballet, leap high into the air with feet gracefully pointed toward the ground. As the dance continues it becomes wilder and is accompanied by croaks, whoops, honks, and trumpeting sounds. As many as 200 cranes have been seen dancing at once.

All cranes have very long windpipes that curl around. These make possible the trumpeting sounds that can often be heard before a flock flies into sight high in the sky. While feeding, cranes croak to one another as though carrying on a conversation.

A crane's nest is a big pile of vegetation just above the water. Male and female incubate the single egg or pair of eggs laid each spring. They care for the chick or chicks together. The chick's call is a high piping whistle. Cranes eat insects, reptiles, rats, mice, grain, seeds, roots, and grasses. They feed their young the same food after partly digesting it.

Creepers

If you see a 5-inch bird the color of bark climbing a tree trunk and you are in a forest in the Northern Hemisphere, you are probably looking at a creeper. The bird probes for bark insects with its slender, down-curved bill while it props itself against the tree trunk with its stiff tail. It works its way upward as though climbing a circular stairway, then flutters down and starts up the next tree.

In spring the male BROWN CREEPER, the only creeper in North America, sings a 5-note song. The female builds a nest hidden under the loose bark of a dead tree. She weaves twigs, bark, ferns, and spider webs together and lines the nest with feathers. She lays 4 to 8 brown-speckled white eggs and with her mate incubates them for 11 days. The young leave the nest 2 weeks after they hatch.

The SHORT-TOED TREE CREEPER of Eurasia and North Africa prefers trees in wooded country, gardens, and parks to those of the forests, and likes hardwoods better than fir, pine, and spruce.

Brown Creeper

Crossbills

Red Crossbill ♂

White-winged Crossbill ♂

These close relatives of sparrows eat the seeds of evergreen and fruit trees. Their crossed bills allow them to remove seeds from pine cones and apples. As their bills move sideways and pry the fruit or cone open, their scooplike tongues snatch the seeds into their mouths.

Crossbills live in the northern forests of Europe, Asia, and North America. The RED CROSSBILL is found on all 3 continents. The WHITE-WINGED CROSSBILL migrates from Canada to suitable places in the United States when pine cones are scarce in its usual territory. The HIMALAYAN CROSSBILL of India, Tibet, and China, lives in mountain forests 15,000 feet above sea level.

Crossbills raise 4 young a year. The chicks are fed on insects and leave the nest with ordinary bills. Soon after they fledge their bills lengthen and become crossed.

Crows

Rooks, jackdaws, ravens, magpies, jays, choughs, and nutcrackers make up a family of bold, noisy birds that take their name from the crows, the noisiest of them all. In addition to all their normal noises, the birds of this group are often mimics and a number have been taught to speak. Do not believe the old story that a crow's tongue should be split. Crows talk with their tongues unhurt.

Jays wear bold patterns of blue, green, yellow, purple, and brown feathers. The rest of the family wear either black or black and white. Male and female of each species are alike. The COMMON RAVEN of Eurasia and northern America has the largest body of any perching bird. It is 26 inches long.

The crow family are all strong flyers, but only a few northern species migrate. The COMMON CROW is in the United States the year round but deserts Canada in the winter and never breeds in Mexico.

These cawing birds are nearly worldwide, occurring everywhere but in New Zealand, the southern tip of South America, and Antarctica. Jays and magpies generally like gardens and woodlands but the SCRUB JAY of Florida seeks palmetto scrubland. The European CHOUGH (rhymes with enough) lives on rocky ledges of high mountains and by the sea, and nests in rock cracks and caves and castle ruins. The ALPINE CHOUGH lives in the Alps and European Pyrenees.

Nutcrackers live in the forests of mountain regions, eat the seeds of fir and other cone-bearing trees, and nest 20 feet or more up in evergreen branches before the snow melts in spring. CLARK'S NUTCRACKER of the Rocky Mountains builds a deep bowl-shaped nest in which the female lays 2 to 6 speckled green eggs. Both parents incubate the eggs in turn for 3 weeks, sometimes in the midst of blizzards. The chicks hatch naked and

Scrub Jay

Common Raven

Clark's Nutcracker

Jackdaw

with eyes closed. They are covered with down within a week, and in 4 weeks are fully feathered and leave the nest able to care for themselves. They hunt for the sweet nuts of the pinyon pine, upon which the parents have fed them.

Most of the black and the black-and-white species of the crow group are not particular about where they live, but the American FISH CROW is. It will live only near the sea. It is a beachcomber on the Atlantic and Gulf Coasts and the tidewaters of the Mississippi. The JACKDAW of Eurasia and northern Africa is most adaptable. If it cannot find a hole in a tree, building, or rock, or an old rabbit burrow, it will build the usual bulky crow-type nest. It likes to be with other jackdaws. It feeds its 2 to 7 young half-digested food from its throat.

The ROOK of Europe nests in colonies. During the winter, it roosts each night in enormous assemblies. From the apparently direct flight of crows comes the expression "as the crow flies." From their eating habits we have "crow bait," meaning worthless meat, for everything vegetable and animal is edible to a crow, even other birds, birds' eggs, and carrion.

All of the crow family are intelligent. It is well known that scarecrows don't scare them after a day or two, and that they recognize a gun and stay out of gun range when they see one. The American common crow makes a fine pet. It can be taught to count to 5 or 6, to open boxes, to fetch like a dog, and many other things. Crows are the mischief-makers of the bird world.

Yellow-billed Cuckoo

Common Cuckoo

Smooth-billed Ani

Roadrunner

Cuckoos

The COMMON CUCKOO of Eurasia says its name over and over. It is loud-voiced, has strange breeding habits, and migrates long distances. The common cuckoos that breed in the forests of Europe fly to Africa, and those that breed in Asia fly to the East Indies for the winter.

All the 42 species of cuckoos in the Old World are parasitic. That is, they lay their eggs in other birds' nests. A female common cuckoo lays about 12 eggs, placing each in a different nest of the species she imposes upon. When she is ready to lay, she goes to the nest of one of several species of smaller songbirds in which the rightful owner has already laid her clutch of eggs. She lifts one of these eggs out in her bill, lays her own egg in its place, and either swallows the

egg she picked up or carries it off and drops it. Cuckoo eggs may be blue or brown, plain or speckled. Each female always lays the same color eggs, and she usually picks a hostess whose eggs are the same color as her own.

The 5 species of cuckoos in North America are not parasitic. They build nests of their own in shrubs or trees in which the females lay 2 to 4 eggs. Both parents incubate the eggs and also feed and protect the young birds.

The 12-inch-long New World YELLOW-BILLED and BLACK-BILLED CUCKOOS live mainly on woolly caterpillars. They eat so many destructive elm and tent caterpillars that they truly help to protect the forests and apple orchards.

The MANGROVE CUCKOO lives in the

mangrove trees on the coasts of tropical America. It breeds on the southernmost Florida Keys. When it calls, it "oos" before it "cucks" as well as after: "oo-cuck-oo."

SMOOTH-BILLED ANIS are also cuckoos of tropical America that have invaded Florida, probably from the West Indies. Anis move, roost, and breed in flocks. They flop along in the air as though their large parrotlike beaks and long drooping tails were a weight too heavy to carry or to balance. They roost at night huddled close to each other like chickens.

The smooth-billed anis build a community nest that flocks of from 8 to 20 birds use together to raise 2 or 3 broods. When the bulky nest is half-built, the female anis start to lay in it, and from then on egg laying, incubation, and care of chicks goes on at one and the same time. Three adult birds may be incubating and feeding chicks while a fourth adds twigs or leaves to the nest. The first brood of chicks often helps to care for the second brood. Anis feed themselves and their young moths, caterpillars, and insects. They are sometimes called "tick-birds" because they eat so many ticks. The smooth-billed ani gives whining calls, rattling tinkles, and squeaky chuckles. The GROOVE-BILLED ANI says "chu-wenk" and sometimes "burp-burp-burp."

The ROADRUNNER is a 22-inch-long cuckoo of southwestern United States and Mexico. Like all cuckoos it has two toes facing forward and two toes facing backward, and so leaves most unusual tracks. It was named for the way it speeds along on foot next to highways at as much as 23 miles an hour. It does not fly well and needs to be quick on its feet to catch rattlesnakes, cotton rats, mice, lizards, tarantulas, and all sorts of insects. The roadrunner's call is more dovelike than other cuckoo calls. It "coos" and "oos" but it doesn't "cuck."

Dickcissels

Curlews

See Snipes

Dickcissels

This member of the sparrow family is dearly loved by the farmers of the prairie states where it breeds. While each pair is raising its 3 to 5 young, a DICKCISSEL family eats about 200 grasshoppers a day. This is one way of controlling insects without poisons. "Dickcissel" is the way the birds' song sounds.

See also: SPARROWS AND RELATED BIRDS

Dippers

North American Dipper

This is an interesting family of small, perching birds which do not migrate. The 4 kinds of dippers live in mountain streams, build their nests behind waterfalls, and eat water insects, fish, and water plants. Dippers spend much of their time underwater walking on creek beds and flying through and over brooks. They have preen glands 10 times larger than those of other perching birds. Oil from these glands keeps the soft, filmy plumage and the heavy down under it waterproofed. The NORTH AMERICAN DIPPER lives in the Rocky Mountains from Alaska to Panama. The COMMON DIPPER bobs up and down in European mountain streams. The PALLAS DIPPER is at home in Japanese mountain torrents and those of mainland northern Asia. Its Japanese name, Kawagarasu, means "river crow." Dippers are also known as "water ouzels."

Dodos

When Portuguese sailors discovered Mauritius Island in the Indian Ocean in 1507, flightless, pigeonlike dodos weighing up to 50 pounds lived there. The dodos ate fruit, seeds, and leaves. They nested on the ground and each female laid only 1 egg each year.

The Portuguese put pigs and monkeys ashore on Mauritius, and ships of other countries also came to the island. The dodos were good to eat and easy to catch, and the visiting sailors and pigs feasted on them. As the monkeys ate each egg as soon as it was laid, the dodos could not raise any young. The last living dodo disappeared about 1680.

21

Domestic Birds

Rock Pigeons (color variations)

Many species of birds have been bred in captivity because they are of some use to man.

The ROCK PIGEON was probably domesticated in Iraq as early as 4500 B.C. for use in religious ceremonies. Ancient Egyptians raised them for food and the Hebrews for sacrifices, as reported in the Bible. The homing instinct of pigeons was known by 1204 B.C. When Rameses III was Pharoah in Egypt he sent 4 pigeons in four directions to carry the news of his coronation. Pigeons carried messages for Caesar and Napoleon. Today pigeons are still raised for racing.

Raising young pigeons called "squabs" for food is a large industry. All domestic pigeons are descendants of the Old World rock pigeon.

Chickens were domesticated soon after the pigeon and also used in religious ceremonies. They were also kept as egg producers. Ancient Greek families kept a cock to wake them in the morning and started raising fighting cocks in about 400 B.C. The Chinese learned how to fatten domestic fowl for the table hundreds of years before the Greeks. The Romans introduced roast chicken into all those parts of Europe

White Domestic Goose

Peking Duck

they conquered.

Indians of Mexico domesticated the turkey long before Columbus discovered the New World. The turkey was brought to Spain in 1498.

Geese were domesticated shortly after chickens. The GRAY-LAG GOOSE of the Old World is the ancestor of most domestic geese. Gray-lag goose eggs often hatch a white gosling. These are called albinos. Albino geese mating with one another eventually produced a race of white domestic geese.

Ducks were domesticated in China about 400 B.C. Today's common white domestic ducks, the PEKINGS, are all descendants of the Chinese birds. The MUSCOVY DUCK, native to South and Central America, was domesticated by the Indians and carried to Europe and Africa by the Portuguese 300 years ago.

Today peafowl are tame birds rather than domestic birds. They were raised for food, especially for festive occasions, during the Middle Ages. But the pea-cock meat is rather tough and not palatable, so the birds were soon moved to the garden as ornamentals.

Quail are domesticated in China, Japan, and Italy and are bred mainly for egg production. Quail eggs have always been a delicacy in those countries, and are now canned in Japan for shipment all over the world.

Ostriches were domesticated in the mid-19th century in Algeria and in southern Africa. They were bred for their plumes. At the end of the century, ostrich farms were established in Florida and California. The plumes were plucked and sold to makers of fans and other feminine furbelows.

Cormorants that fish for their masters and falcons that hunt for their masters are not rightfully domestic birds. While they are tamed, they are captured from the wild, not bred in captivity.

See also: CHICKENS; CORMORANTS; GUINEA FOWL; HAWKS; PHEASANTS; PIGEONS; TURKEYS; WATERFOWL

♂
Muscovy Duck

Dovekies

See Auks

Doves

See Pigeons

Ducks

See Domestic Birds; Waterfowl

Harpy Eagle

Eagles

All through history nations, rulers, and conquerors have chosen an eagle as an emblem. The royal house of ancient Babylonia used an eagle as its symbol of state 6,000 years ago. This was probably the GOLDEN EAGLE known north of the equator the world around, and often called "the king of the birds." The golden eagle was displayed on the banners carried by Caesar's, Charlemagne's, and Napoleon's armies. It became the emblem of many modern nations.

The BALD EAGLE, whose white-feathered head makes it look bald, is the national bird of the United States. It is found throughout North America except in arctic and desert regions. Its favorite food is fish which it sometimes obtains by forcing a successful osprey to drop its catch. So swift is the bald eagle in flight that it has the fish in its talons before it has fallen more than a foot or two. Usually bald eagles catch fish swimming on the surface of the water or pick up dead fish washed ashore. They

Golden Eagle

Bald Eagle

also eat small mammals and ducks wounded during the hunting season.

Eagles mate for life and repair and use the same bulky nest, on a cliff or on top of a high tree, year after year. The female and her smaller mate take turns incubating their 2 dull white eggs and feeding their young. It takes 6 weeks for the eggs to hatch, and the eaglets remain in the nest for another 3 months. Adult eagles clean the catch before carrying it to their nestlings.

An adult female bald eagle weighs about 9 pounds and a female golden eagle about the same. As an eagle cannot lift anything heavier than itself, all the stories of eagles carrying away live children are untrue.

The largest eagle in the world is the HARPY EAGLE of tropical Central and South America. A female may weigh as much as 15 pounds. Harpy eagles live in the tall rain forests and hunt marmosets, sloths, and large jungle birds. *See also:* HAWKS

25

Egrets

See Herons

Emus

*See Ostriches and
Other Ratite Birds*

Falcons

♀
Lesser Kestrel

White Gyrfalcon

These birds of prey have long pointed wings, large black eyes above sharply hooked short beaks, and longish legs with strong hooked claws on their very long toes. Their 2 to 6 eggs are always spotted with reddish-brown splotches. They do not build nests, but lay on cliff ledges and in the old nests of crows and other birds. A European species, the LESSER KESTREL, breeds in colonies of from 15 to 25 pairs and up to 100 pairs, in holes in old town walls or rotting trees. But most falcons nest by themselves.

Falcons hunt their prey—mammals, birds, reptiles, and large insects—from high on a perch or while flying far above the ground. When the GYRFALCON swoops upon prey, its flight is faster than that of any other bird in the world. It can dive at a speed of 175 miles an hour. The gyrfalcon is undoubtedly one of the falcons that inspired men thousands of years ago to catch young falcons and train them to hunt and bring their prey back to the falconer.

Modern weapons out-dated hunting with falcons several hundred years ago as a way of getting game for the table. But it is still a popular sport in many countries and is preserved by the Imperial Household in Japan for its historical interest.

Feathers

Birds evolved from a scaly reptilian ancestor and they still have scales on their legs. Some scientists believe that feathers developed from scales, but no one really knows. Feathers, scales, horns, antlers, hair, claws, and nails are all formed from a horny material called keratin. Feathers, like hair, toenails, and fingernails, have no feeling and can be cut and trimmed without causing pain to a bird, but a trimmed feather does not keep growing like a trimmed nail. When a feather reaches its fixed size it stops growing.

Feathers are much more important to a bird than hair and nails are to man. Feathers aid flight. Wing and tail feathers do the work of propeller and rudder on an airplane. They give a bird lift, forward push, and a way to steer.

Feathers also protect birds from temperature changes. By trapping air against a bird's skin they provide insulation against heat in summer and against cold in winter. Many birds in cold climates wear more feathers than birds in warm places. A $5\frac{3}{4}$-inch WHITE-THROATED SPARROW grows as many as 2710 feathers before winter in New England and loses nearly half in summer.

Feathers do not grow all over a bird's body, but just in special places on the skin. They grow in these "feather tracts" so that they overlap the bare skin between them. Each species has its own design of feather tracts, but all have tracts on the head, down the middle back, and on either side of the breast and belly. A bird keeps its feathers in order by dipping its bill in the preen gland just above its tail and smoothing its feathers with the preen oil.

After the breeding season is over in summer, most birds molt. They lose their old worn feathers and grow new ones. Some birds molt twice a year, like the INDIGO BUNTING that changes its winter plumage in the spring for courting feathers. The WILLOW PTARMIGAN wears brown feathers in summer and white in winter. During its spring molt it is half brown and half white and matches its surroundings, a patchwork of melting snow and brownish ground.

Most birds lose wing and tail feathers one at a time on either side so they are always in balance and can fly. Several waterfowl and some other birds molt all their wing feathers at once and cannot fly until the new ones grow in.

Birds wear different kinds of feathers. The feathers that give a bird its shape, the contour feathers, have a stiff spine, the "shaft," with a "vane" on either side. Down feathers are very short, soft feathers without stiff shafts. They are worn under the contour feathers and by newly hatched chicks. Plumes are long, fancy feathers. They are worn by egrets when courting and breeding and by male birds of paradise and ostriches the year round. Many other birds wear ornamental plumes.

Scientists have made the following counts of the number of feathers on a bird: a WHISTLING SWAN in November, 25,216; a PIED-BILLED GREBE in December, 15,016; a PINTAIL DUCK in January, 14,914; a MOCKINGBIRD in March, 3,297; a CARDINAL in July, 3,183.

Finches

When the male of a species of American sparrow has red, pink, or yellow feathers mixed with his brown-and-white sparrow plumage, he and his mate, who does not have the bright feathers, are usually called finches. The AMERICAN GOLDFINCH breeds in southern Canada and northern United States and winters all through the United States. Its song is long and clear and sweet. The PURPLE FINCH lives in open woods and gardens from central Canada in summer to the Gulf of Mexico in winter. It does not occur in the Great Plains. The bright feathers of the male bird are red, with just a tinge of purple. His courting song on his northern breeding grounds is music as fine as that of any canary. Some Old World sparrows of various colors are also called finches.

See also: SPARROWS AND RELATED BIRDS

Flamingos

A flamingo has a large down-curved beak, a corkscrew neck, broomstick legs, and salmon-pink feathers. Adult flamingos feed with their heads hanging down in front of their stamping feet. The upside-down upper bill stays still and the bottom bill moves against it to pick up small shellfish disturbed by the feet. With the help of the tongue, the sand is strained out before the catch is swallowed, shells and all.

Young flamingos when they hatch are hardly as big as their parents' strange bills. Their first food is a sort of shellfish chowder the old birds dribble into their small straight open bills. They also eat the shells from which they hatched. At the end of 3 weeks the bills of flamingo chicks start to grow and to turn down. The young soon begin to feed in the same way their parents do.

Flamingos often fly at sunset and sunrise. Then their brilliant color makes them almost invisible against the rosy sky. The AMERICAN FLAMINGO of the New World tropics is so like the GREATER FLAMINGO of the Old World tropics that many scientists believe they are the same species.

Kingbirds, phoebes, and wood pewees as well as flycatchers are part of this family of 367 species of perching birds. They live in the forests and grasslands of the Americas. Thirty-one species live in North America. Most are small-bodied birds less than 6 inches long, but the SCISSOR-TAILED FLYCATCHER's 9-inch tail makes its total length 13 inches. The BLACK-HEADED TODY-FLYCATCHER of tropical South America is only 3½ inches long including its tail.

Flycatchers are often called "tyrants." The EASTERN and WESTERN KINGBIRDS behave like tyrants. They drive all other birds away from their territory, fearlessly attacking the much larger crows and hawks. They eat bees and pay no attention to their stings.

Flycatchers sit upright on a perch watching and waiting until an insect comes by. Then they swoop on their prey in the air or on the ground, as swiftly as falcons stoop to theirs.

Flycatchers have many loud calls but little song. The EASTERN WOOD PEWEE whistles "pee-o-wee" all day long from high in the trees and looks much like the EASTERN PHOEBE that calls "phee-bee" constantly. Phoebes usually live near running water and build their nests on bridge supports and the ledges of streamside cliffs. SAY'S PHOEBE of western North America sings "phee" but ends its call with "your."

Most flycatchers can raise the feathers on the tops of their heads into crests and do so when courting or when disturbed. The GREAT CRESTED FLYCATCHER that breeds in eastern North America has more crest than most flycatchers. The great crested flycatcher builds a bulky nest in a tree hole or bird box of roots, grass, fiber, a snake's shed skin, and shiny odds and ends like cellophane, silver paper, and onion skins. She incubates her 5 to 6 eggs by herself, but the male helps her feed insects to the nestlings. Its loud calls are heard in the tropics in winter. Cotingas and silky flycatchers are other families of flycatchers of the American tropics.

Flickers

See Woodpeckers

Flycatchers

Scissor-tailed Flycatcher
♂

Great Crested Flycatcher

Eastern Phoebe

Eastern Kingbird

Frigate-Birds

♀

Magnificent Frigate Birds

♂

These soaring birds of the tropic seas never rest on the water. All five species hang in the sky for hours on motionless wings with forked tails spread wide. Frigate-birds obtain their food by snatching fish that swim near the surface. They also force terns and other birds to give up their catch.

On some Pacific islands the natives use frigate-birds to carry messages from island to island. Sailors call them "man-o'-war hawks."

The MAGNIFICENT FRIGATE-BIRD of the New World, like all male frigate-birds, wears a heart-shaped balloonlike red pouch on his throat when courting. He can blow it up whenever he wishes and keep it inflated for hours. Frigate-birds nest in trees and on the tops of bushes on oceanic islands. Each pair raises a single young bird each year.

Fulmars

See Petrels

Gannets

In Old German the gannet's name means "sea goose." The three kinds that live in temperate seas have kept the name: the NORTHERN GANNET of the North Atlantic, the CAPE GANNET of South African waters, and the AUSTRALIAN GANNET of the seas around Australia and New Zealand.

The six species that live in tropic seas were called boobies—meaning stupid—by sailors on the sailing ships of long ago. It was not smart of the boobies to land on the ships, but how were they to know the sailors would whack them

Blue-faced Booby

Brown Booby

over the head and make stew of them? The stew tasted like fish because the food of all gannets is fish and squid. But it was a welcome change from salt pork and sea biscuit. Boobies follow ships to catch the flying fish that fly away from their bows. They dive from the air for other fish. The BLUE-FACED BOOBY or MASKED BOOBY, the BROWN BOOBY, and the RED-FOOTED BOOBY nest on various tropical islands the world around including the West Indies. They are sometimes seen off the southernmost coasts of the United States.

Gallinaceous Birds

The Latin for rooster is *gallus*, and gallinaceous means "to do with poultry." Gallinaceous birds are ground birds related to the chickens. They include turkeys, pheasants, grouse, quails, guinea fowl, partridges, the chachalacas of Texas and Central and South America, the strange hoatzin, and the mound builders of the southwest Pacific. The jungle fowls of southeastern Asia and their descendants, our chickens, are members of the pheasant family, the commonest of gallinaceous birds.

Chachalaca

Jungle Fowl ♂

Gallinules
See Rails

Geese
See Waterfowl

Gnatcatchers

The BLUE-GRAY GNATCATCHER, the GOLDEN-CROWNED KINGLET, and the RUBY-CROWNED KINGLET of North America are Old World warblers, a family found in woodlands around the globe. These 4-inch-long insect-eaters live almost entirely on harmful plant lice and their eggs. High in a tree the blue-gray gnatcatcher builds a nest of down and fine plant fibers tied with spider webs and trimmed with bits of a gray air plant, or lichen, that grows on bark and rock. The nest is so small it will fit into a teacup with room to spare. Before the trees leaf out in spring it holds 5 brown-speckled blue eggs the size of navy beans. Using the same materials the kinglets build a ball-shaped nest with a top entrance in which the kinglet female lays 8 or 9 eggs.

Golden-crowned Kinglet

Ruby-crowned Kinglet

Blue-gray Gnatcatcher

Grackles

See Blackbirds

Grebes

The 18 different kinds of grebes have thick, waterproof plumage. Their dark feathers are satiny and their white feathers glisten. Grebes have an odd habit. They eat and feed their chicks some of their own body feathers. Nobody knows why. Their usual food is small fish, shellfish, insects, and some water weeds.

A grebe's nest is a heap of wet, rotting water plants floating in shallow water. It may or may not be anchored to growing plant stems. Grebes lay a clutch of 2 to 8 chalky-white eggs which are soon stained brown by the nesting material which the old birds pull over them to hide them when leaving the nest. The nestlings hatch covered with soft down.

Red-necked Grebe

They are immediately able to swim and can climb onto a parent bird's back and cling while the adult dives and swims under water.

Grebes use their large flat scalloped feet as paddles on and under water. They are completely aquatic birds and even court in the water. When a pair of GREAT CRESTED GREBES dive and rise in a courting dance they pose upright like penguins. They flash their shining white bellies while their feet patter over the water. The great crested grebe ranges from the lakes of northern Eurasia through those of Africa, Australia, and New Zealand.

The EARED GREBE often nests in colonies in marshy lakes in western North America. It winters along the Pacific Coast from Washington State to Guatemala. It also occurs throughout Eurasia. The RED-NECKED GREBE breeds on forest lakes across northern North America and Eurasia. The little LAKE TITICACA GREBE lives only in that one lake high in the Peruvian Andes, because it cannot fly.

Grosbeaks

Grosbeak is the name of a number of American sparrows whose bills are heavier and stronger than those of their relatives. The ROSE-BREASTED GROSBEAK is a fine singer of northeastern hardwood forests and has adapted to life in suburban gardens. The EVENING GROSBEAK breeds across southern Canada and in western mountains. It comes to feeding shelves for sunflower seeds in the winter months in the United States as well as in Canada, but avoids the southeast. The PINE GROSBEAK lives in northern evergreen forests around the world, and the BLUE GROSBEAK is a favorite songster of the southern United States.

See also: SPARROWS AND RELATED BIRDS

Blue Grosbeak
♂

Evening Grosbeak
♂

Rose-breasted Grosbeak
♂

Grouse

These ground birds live on the open prairies, high mountain slopes, the arctic tundras, and the steppes of Eurasia. They are favorites of the hunters of the Northern Hemisphere.

The SPRUCE GROUSE is hunted in Alaska and Canada and the RUFFED GROUSE in Canada and the northern United States. In the sagebrush country of the west the SAGE GROUSE is a favorite. In north and central Eurasia, the CAPERCAILLIE, the BLACK GROUSE, and the HAZEL HEN delight the hunter. Most

Rock Ptarmigan
(summer plumage)   (winter plumage)

Greater Prairie Chicken
♂

cock grouse are from 10 to 15 inches long, but the capercaillie is a turkey-sized 34 inches and the sage grouse only 6 inches smaller. Female grouse are never quite as big as males.

One grouse, the HEATH HEN, once lived along the eastern coast of America from Maine to Virginia. It was so popular with hunters and housewives that it was hunted right out of existence. The heath hen was an eastern type of GREATER PRAIRIE CHICKEN. GREATER and LESSER PRAIRIE CHICKENS survive in the west but are becoming rare. They are now protected and so may survive on refuges established just for them.

In a great circle around the pole, WILLOW and ROCK PTARMIGAN have provided food for American and Icelandic Eskimos, European Laplanders, Siberian tribes, and Mongolian nomads. Sportsmen in the

British Isles hunt the willow ptarmigan which they call the RED GROUSE. The rock ptarmigan is hunted in the European Alps, the Pyrenees Mountains of France and Spain, the Urals of Russia, and the Japanese Alps.

The willow ptarmigan and the rock ptarmigan nest within the Arctic Circle. Their feet and legs are completely covered with feathers which are as warm as wool socks in below-zero temperatures. During heavy snows ptarmigans find a warm sleeping place by flying straight into soft drifts of snow. The snow closes behind them and no telltale tracks are left to guide a hungry arctic fox. In winter they eat twigs of willow, alder, and other arctic plants.

♂
Ruffed Grouse

The 18 species of grouse have very similar habits. The courtship dances of the males in spring are very elaborate and noisy. Some gather into groups where they bow, spread their tails, droop their wings, and at the same time crow, sing, or give booming cries. All cocks have courting ornaments—bright wattles or bare colored skin above the eye or on the neck, and also tufts of feathers to display. Some, like greater and lesser prairie chickens, puff out balloonlike air sacs on their necks. Some grouse court alone from a perch on a tree. The ruffed grouse courts from a log and makes a drumming noise by moving his wings against the air. The ruffed and the spruce grouse take only one mate, but most cock grouse take a harem of from 2 to 15 hens. Grouse hens each build a nest and incubate from 2 to 22 eggs. They raise the chicks without the cock's help. The chicks may stay with the mother until the following spring. *See also:* FEATHERS; GALLINACEOUS BIRDS

Guillemots

See Auks

Guinea fowl

Vulturine Guinea Fowl

Helmeted Guinea Fowl

Africa, south of the Sahara Desert, is the home of 7 kinds of guinea fowl. They feed and nest on the ground but roost in trees. They like each other's company and move around in flocks of a hundred or more birds. In the breeding season the mated pairs stay by themselves. The hen lays from 12 to 30 eggs, which she incubates for 3 to 4 weeks, in a ground nest. The young run around as soon as they are hatched.

The VULTURINE GUINEA FOWL, 30 inches long, is the largest species. The HELMETED GUINEA FOWL is the ancestor of the farmers' birds that have been carried to every continent. *See also:* DOMESTIC BIRDS; GALLINACEOUS BIRDS

Arctic Tern

Black Tern

Sooty Tern

Gulls

Sea birds' feathers are generally white, black, gray, or brown. They blend with the sea and sky. The 43 kinds of gulls and 39 kinds of terns wear these colors in various combinations, but their bills and legs are often yellow, red, or orange. Scientists put gulls and terns in the same family although gulls differ from terns greatly in appearance and behavior.

Gulls are stouter, wider-winged, and longer-legged than terns. Terns are called "sea swallows" because of their slender grace in flight. Gulls, although they fly strongly and soar to great heights, do not make such a picture of slender grace. Gulls' bills are strongly hooked; terns' bills are pointed. The color of the plumage of 1- and 2-year-old gulls differs so much from that of the adult birds that they look like different species. The color of the plumage of young terns differs very little, if at all, from that of the adult birds.

Gulls are scavengers and tidy up after litterbugs. They eat refuse from ships and at wharfs in all the harbors of the world, and at garbage dumps and picnic grounds. They eat the young and eggs of other birds, and all sorts of vegetable matter. HERRING GULLS and RING-BILLED GULLS of North American coasts and inland waters eat shellfish and cleverly break the clam or snail shell by drop-ping it from the air onto rocks, flat-roofed beach houses, or a paved highway.

Gulls are fine fishermen but only work at fishing or insect-hunting when hand-outs are scarce and hunger drives them. Terns on the other hand are choosy about their food and like to have it alive. They dive from the air to catch minnows and squid below the surface of the water and usually disdain any other food. Inland terns often catch insects on the wing.

Both gulls and terns nest in colonies on offshore islands and in inland lakes and marshes. Gulls usually build nests and lay 2 to 4 eggs. Most terns lay their 1 to 3 eggs on the bare sand. The NODDY TERN, a tropical ocean bird, is known in

North America only on Florida's Dry Tortugas Islands. It builds a twig platform in shrubby bushes to hold its single brown-speckled egg. The BLACK TERN of inland waters lays its 3 eggs on matted canes, floating vegetable matter, old muskrat houses, or old nests of other birds. It places a bit of dry plant material on the spot before laying to keep the eggs out of water. FORSTER'S TERN selects the same nesting sites but builds a substantial nest lined with fine grasses to hold its 3 eggs. Pairs of GREAT BLACK-BACKED GULLS breed alone or in small colonies on islands or coasts of the North Atlantic and the Arctic Ocean from Labrador eastward to western Russia and winter south to North Carolina and the Mediterranean Sea.

Terns are champion long-distance flyers. The LEAST TERN breeds in the temperate parts of the Northern Hemisphere and winters south to Africa and Australia, and to South America. The ARCTIC TERN breeds on islands in northern North America and Europe and winters in the southern oceans south to the Antarctic. Arctic terns that hatch in Labrador travel to South Africa's coast for the first time when they are 3 months old. They make this trip every August for the rest of their lives, and they can live to be 29 years old. Every spring they fly from South Africa back to Labrador to breed.

Gulls and terns are noisy. Many gulls have harsh voices and croak like crows. They also cry shrilly and scream. The KITTIWAKE, a gull of the Northern Hemisphere, screams when disturbed but also calls pleasantly "kit-ti-wake." SOOTY TERNS cry all day and all night, too, and so are known as "wide-a-wakes." These terns share the range of the noddy terns and breed in the same colonies. Sooty terns spend about 4 months on their nesting grounds. For the other 8 months of the year they remain at sea on the wing. As they cannot swim and never alight on the water, they must be able to rest or sleep as they soar. Sooty terns can live to be 31 years old.

Black-legged Kittiwake

Great Black-backed Gull

Herring Gull

Bataleur Eagle

Swallow-tailed Kite

Hawks

True hawks, eagles, kites, and harriers are all part of this family of 205 species of broad-winged birds of prey. They are found in all lands except Antarctica and the Sahara Desert. They hunt from a perch or from the air, and their marvelous eyes can see small creatures far away. They capture live animals in their strong hooked claws and tear large prey apart with their short hooked bills. Except for the harriers, male and female hawks look alike, but females are always larger than males. The hawk family all wear feathers on the upper parts of their rather long legs. When the birds perch or walk they look as though they were wearing feather pants.

The most graceful of the North American hawks are the kites. They sail through the air with ease. The WHITE-TAILED KITE was once a familiar bird from South Carolina and California to Argentina. Now this mouse-eater is a rare bird in the United States. The SWALLOW-TAILED KITE, a lizard-, frog-, snake-, and dragonfly-eater once known from the Canadian border to Argentina, is now only seen once in a while in the states bordering the Gulf of Mexico. These two kites are useful to mankind in controlling mice and snakes. They have been destroyed in the United States by illegal shooting. The EVERGLADES KITE was reduced to 90 individuals in 1969. Draining the Florida marshes is destroying this once plentiful bird by killing the apple snails that are its only food.

The GOSHAWK and the MARSH HAWK are, like the GOLDEN EAGLE, birds of the Northern Hemisphere, breeding in Eurasia and North America. Goshawks hunt small mammals and birds in the forest. The marsh hawk is the only harrier in North America. In Eurasia lives the similar HEN HARRIER. Harriers hunt from a few feet above the ground tipping from side to side as they search for rats, snakes, frogs, small birds, and large insects. The marsh hawk feasts on cotton rats while migrating and also while wintering in the southern states.

The Latin word for hawk is *buteo*. It is the scientific name of 13 hawks that often sit on posts or telegraph poles, and hunt food by circling high in the sky and diving down on their prey. Common through North America is the ROUGH-LEGGED HAWK that lives on ground

Marsh Hawk

Cooper's Hawk

Goshawk

Red-tailed Hawk

squirrels, pocket gophers, and mice, and the RED-TAILED HAWK that pounces on snakes, lizards, frogs, crayfish, insects, mice, squirrels, rabbits, and shrews. The RED-SHOULDERED HAWK of the eastern United States and California likes the same food as the red-tailed hawk.

All these hawks are unjustly accused of taking the farmers' poultry. The real thief is usually one of the long-legged hawks, the COOPER'S HAWK or the SHARP-SHINNED HAWK. Those are widespread in North America and are found in Florida and in Central America in the winter. The sharp-shinned hawk is not much bigger than an American robin, about 10 inches long.

Largest of the hawk family are the eagles, and the BATALEUR EAGLE of Africa is the gentlest, the most amusing, and the gayest of these big birds of prey. The bataleur eagle has a patch of leathery red skin above its bright yellow beak that matches its red feet, back, and tail. In flight it soars and does somersaults in the air. It courts with aerial acrobatics, moving its wings so that they make a sound like knocking on wood and cawing at the same time. The bataleur is

very fond of snakes but will attack all sorts of animals, even a small deer. It is a clown in the air but quite dignified on the ground. It will come to a garden for food scraps. It always bows to its food several times before eating. It is easily tamed, makes a fine pet, and soon stops hunting if well fed. It will fly for pleasure and exercise but returns home of its own accord.

Except for the ground-nesting harriers and some kites, the hawk family nest high in trees, on rock ledges, or cliffs. They build bulky nests of sticks and bark and often use them year after year. Male and female mate for life and work together to raise from 1 to 6 chicks a year. The eggs are incubated for 30 to 60 days. The downy young hatch blind and helpless and cannot leave the nest for at least a month. In some large species the young do not fly for 4 months. The parent birds protect their nestlings fearlessly and do not hesitate to attack an intruder with claws and curling nails. The SPARROW HAWK and the PIGEON HAWK of America are falcons. *See also:* CARACARAS; EAGLES; FALCONS; OSPREYS

39

Herons

Black-crowned Night Heron

Cattle Egret

The quiet shallow waters of rivers, marshes, lakes and seas of the warmer lands of the world are home to 63 kinds of herons. Here these birds wade and catch fish, crabs, insects, amphibians, reptiles, and rats. Using their straight long bills as spears, they pierce their prey and then swallow it whole. Indigestible fish scales, bones, feathers, and fur are rolled into neat little balls in the stomach. The birds cough up and spit out these balls.

Male and female herons wear the same dress and grow the same courting plumage. Under their contour feathers, they have rows of an odd sort of down that flakes off into powder. Herons dip their bills into this powder and with it clean their plumage, removing fish oil, dirt and slime.

The heron family includes the bitterns, night herons, egrets, and the herons themselves. Herons that breed in northern Eurasia and America migrate in winter. Tropical herons do not migrate.

From American fresh-water marshes in spring from dusk to midnight comes a thumping, pumping sound, a mixture of a croak and air escaping from the loosely held nipple of a toy balloon. This is the mating call of the male AMERICAN BITTERN, one kind of heron. Because of its call the bird is nicknamed "Thunder Pumper," "Stake Driver," and "Plum Pudd'n" which it seems to say.

East of the Mississippi and in California the LEAST BITTERN lives hidden in tall salt- and fresh-water grasses and sedges. This is the smallest of the herons, an 11-inch-long bird. Its call is a gutteral "coo" repeated 4 to 6 times. The calls of bitterns can be heard a quarter of a mile away. Bitterns build platform nests a few feet above the water. The parents raise 4 or 5 young each spring. They do not nest in colonies. In Eurasia the COMMON and the LITTLE BITTERN take the place of the American and least bittern and have

Little Blue Heron ♂

Great Blue Heron ♂

Reddish Egret ♂

American Bittern

similar habits. Bitterns migrate southward in winter, silently at night.

The almost world-wide BLACK-CROWNED NIGHT HERON and the YELLOW-CROWNED NIGHT HERON get their names from their habit of roosting and sleeping during the day and fishing at night. In Japan the black-crowned night heron is called the "Goi sagi" meaning "heron of the fifth imperial rank." The Emperor Daigo knighted it in the year 930 A.D. because of its beauty and tameness.

Largest of the heron family are the GREAT BLUE HERON of North and Central America and the GRAY HERON of Eurasia and Africa. They are 38 inches long from bill tip to tail tip, but stand over 4 feet tall on their long legs. The GREAT WHITE HERON of southern Florida is just as tall. The LITTLE GREEN HERON is found in the same places as the least bittern and is a little larger. The LITTLE BLUE HERON is white for the first year of its life and is then confused with the SNOWY EGRET during the winter months when egrets do not wear their fancy plumes.

A number of herons are called "egrets," which is also the name for the delicate, airy plumes both male and female wear during the breeding season. The SNOWY

Snowy Egret

EGRET, COMMON EGRET, and REDDISH EGRET were killed for their beautiful plumes during the 18th and 19th centuries. Audubon Societies and the American Ornithologists Union raised money to pay wardens to guard the egrets and campaigned for laws to protect them. They were successful and egrets are fairly plentiful today in North America.

One strange egret is a newcomer to North America. The CATTLE EGRET is a native of Africa. Shortly after World War I this bird crossed the Atlantic Ocean and settled in British Guiana in northeastern South America. From there it wandered northward. In the early 1950's it appeared in Florida. Today it is widespread in the eastern United States where it follows cattle to eat the insects they disturb as they browse.

Herons, night herons, and egrets nest in colonies in trees where they build flimsy, shallow nests of sticks. The 3 to 6 eggs are incubated by male and female. The downy young are fed half-digested food by both parents. A heronry is a very noisy place. The adults squawk and croak and the chicks squeak. After some years a heron colony usually has to move. The heron droppings and spilled fish over-fertilize the trees, and they eventually die.

Hoatzins

The hoatzin is most interesting to scientists as a sort of missing link between prehistoric birds and modern birds. When a hoatzin chick hatches it has 2 claws on each wing like ARCHAEOPTERYX, a bird that lived 130 million years ago. The chick uses its wing claws with its feet claws to cling to tree limbs. It loses the wing claws as soon as feathers grow. The chick can swim when hatched. The hoatzin is the only gallinaceous bird that regularly swims.

Hoatzins live on the banks of rivers in northern South America and build frail nests over the water. They eat and feed their 2 to 3 chicks rubbery leaves of a tall arum tree the natives call the "mucca-mucca." Hoatzins have enormous crops and weak flying muscles. They eat their way to the top of a mucca-mucca tree, flop into the air, and half glide, half fall to the bottom of another. They cannot really fly. Hoatzins have hairlike feather eyelashes.
See also: GALLINACEOUS BIRDS

Honeyguides

Black-throated Honeyguide

This is a family of 11 species of small drab birds, 9 in Africa and 2 in Asia. In spite of their name, they do not eat honey. The BLACK-THROATED HONEY-GUIDE of Africa south of the Sahara Desert is probably the most famous small bird of that continent. It eats beeswax and can digest it. It cannot open the bees' nest by itself, so it seeks a honey badger or a man, which it "guides" or leads to the honey tree with its call. The badger or the man opens the bees' nest and gets the honey, and the bird gets the wax. The black-throated honey-guide has an unusually tough skin and a musty odor that protect it from bee stings.

Honeyguides lay their eggs in other birds' nests as do the common cuckoo and the brown-headed cowbird. The honeyguides peck holes in the eggs of the rightful owner of the nest where they lay their eggs.

Hoopoes

An old legend says the hoopoe was given his crown by King Solomon. It was a reward for shading that monarch from the desert sun with its outspread wings. Hoopoes appear to be very conscious of their crowns, raising and lowering them as they feed on the ground and as they fly, wavering like butterflies. They eat grubs and termites, digging into garbage and manure to find them. The hoopoe's name comes from the male's low penetrating call, "hoop-hoop," repeated over and over.

Hoopoes nest in holes in trees, banks and in ruined buildings. The female incubates the 4 to 6 blue or green eggs for 18 days, rarely leaving the nest. The male brings her food and, for some days after the chicks hatch, the male brings food to mother and young. Hoopoes are devoted parents but bad housekeepers. Their nest-holes are so dirty they can be traced by their horrid odor.

44

Hornbills

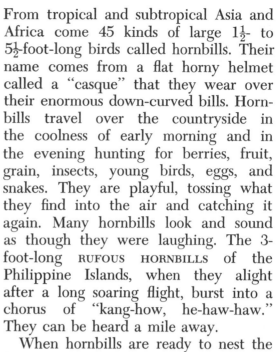

Great Hornbill

Black-casqued Hornbill

From tropical and subtropical Asia and Africa come 45 kinds of large 1½- to 5½-foot-long birds called hornbills. Their name comes from a flat horny helmet called a "casque" that they wear over their enormous down-curved bills. Hornbills travel over the countryside in the coolness of early morning and in the evening hunting for berries, fruit, grain, insects, young birds, eggs, and snakes. They are playful, tossing what they find into the air and catching it again. Many hornbills look and sound as though they were laughing. The 3-foot-long RUFOUS HORNBILLS of the Philippine Islands, when they alight after a long soaring flight, burst into a chorus of "kang-how, he-haw-haw." They can be heard a mile away.

When hornbills are ready to nest the female enters the nesting hole in a hollow tree and seals herself in, using her own droppings as plaster. She remains in her prison for 28 to 40 days to incubate the eggs and 2 to 4 weeks longer until the chicks are half-grown. The length of time depends on the species of hornbill. All during the imprisonment she sticks the tip of her bill out of a slit to dispose of her droppings. Through the same slit the male feeds the female and the 2 to 4 chicks. Scientists believe the hornbills adapted this strange way of nesting to protect the eggs and young from bands of monkeys. While the female is in her prison she molts all her feathers and grows new ones. When she comes out she is fat and so stiff she can hardly fly.

The HELMETED HORNBILL of tropical Asia is over 5 feet long, including a 3-foot tail. This bird of the tall trees of the evergreen forests calls with a series of whoops, closer and closer together, that ends in a harsh cackling laugh. The GREAT HORNBILL of southeastern Asia often covers itself with bright yellow oil from its preening gland. The wings of the BLACK-CASQUED HORNBILL of Africa sound like a puffing steam engine when it flies.

45

Streamertail Hummingbird ♂

Blue-throated Hummingbird ♂

Ruby Topaz Hummingbird ♂

Rufous Hummingbird ♂

Hummingbirds

If emeralds, rubies, sapphires, amethysts, and all the other gemstones grew wings and flew, they might rival the gleaming, glistening male hummingbirds. Many hummingbirds are named for gemstones—the RUBY TOPAZ, the CARIB EMERALD, the AMETHYST-THROATED and the RUBY-THROATED HUMMINGBIRDS. In the 19th century, millions of hummingbird skins were shipped to Europe from South America and the West Indies to be worn as ornaments. But hummingbirds, fortunately, did not last as well as gemstones. If this had not been so, many of the 319 kinds of hummingbirds would have long since been extinct.

Hummingbirds are all small birds. The CUBAN BEE HUMMINGBIRD of the West Indies, only $2\frac{1}{4}$ inches long from the tip of its bill to the tip of its tail, is the smallest bird in the world. It weighs only as much as one-quarter teaspoon of sugar. No hummingbird has a body more than 4 inches long, but the GIANT HUMMINGBIRD of South America's Andes Mountains is 8 inches long when a 2-inch bill and a 2-inch tail are measured in. A 5-inch bill and a 1-inch tail make the SWORD-BILLED HUMMINGBIRD of northwestern South America $8\frac{1}{2}$ inches long.

The RUFOUS HUMMINGBIRD breeds as far north as southern Alaska and the CHILEAN FIRE-CROWN breeds as far south as Tierra del Fuego, the southern tip of South America. But more kinds of hum-

mingbirds occur in the tropics and subtropics than elsewhere. Species that nest in the north, like the 3-inch ruby-throated hummingbird of eastern United States, migrate south in winter. The ruby-throated hummingbird flies at least 500 miles nonstop across the Gulf of Mexico on its way down to Brazil to spend the winter. It can fly at 30 miles an hour. The BLUE-THROATED HUMMINGBIRD of Mexico also nests in the mountains of southwestern Texas, New Mexico, and Arizona.

The "hum" of hummingbirds is made by their swiftly-beating wings. The hummers' wings move so fast that they are a blur. In recent years special cameras and equipment were invented to photograph flying hummingbirds. The pictures prove that hummingbirds can fly backward as well as forward and can remain poised in the air. Hummingbirds hover like helicopters and whirl their wings like helicopter rotors.

Small soft insects, ants, flies and flower nectar are hummingbird food. Hovering in the air before a blossom the hummingbird inserts its slender pointed bill into the heart of the flower. The tongue darts beyond the bill and brings in insects and sweet juices, and sometimes a bee. Most hummingbird bills are straight but a few curve downward like that of the EMERALD-THROATED HUMMINGBIRD of the West Indies. Curved bills are probably useful in sipping from a curved flower tube.

Hummingbirds will come to a tube of sugar-water hung in the garden. They prefer a mixture of no more than one part sugar with nine parts water. If it is colored red, pink, orange, or purple, the favorite colors of the hummers, it will be more attractive to them.

When the males of any bird family have gayer plumage than the females, they are apt to let the females raise the family alone. This is so among hummingbirds. The females weave dainty open cup-shaped nests of plant down and spider webs with bits of moss on the outside. Each female lays 2 pure white eggs less than $\frac{1}{4}$ inch long and incubates them for 14 to 19 days. The young hatch naked and do not leave the nest for about 3 weeks. Hummingbirds cannot walk, so the young must be able to fly from the nest. To rest hummingbirds perch on slender twigs and stems.

Sword-billed Hummingbird ♂

Ruby-throated Hummingbirds ♂ ♀

Giant Hummingbird ♂

Ibises

The best known of the 22 kinds of these big 20- to 40-inch, long-legged wading birds is the GLOSSY IBIS from Eurasia, Africa, Australia, and southernmost United States and Central America. Ibises like to be with one another, but they do not mix with other birds except sometimes when feeding. They nest in groups, they fly in groups, and they roost in trees at night in groups. Occasionally when only a few glossy ibises are flying they join the WHITE IBIS that breeds from the southeastern United States to Peru. Ibises fly with their necks straight out in front and their legs trailing behind.

The most beautiful ibis in the New World is the SCARLET IBIS of South America. It has been slaughtered for its feathers and its meat. The native Indians of the countries where it lives like its oily, fishy flavor.

Ibises are usually rather quiet birds but when they call they sound like grunting pigs or they croak harshly. Their down-curved bills are excellent tools for catching animal life in the mud. Most ibises have patches of bare skin on their heads and necks. The WATTLED IBIS of Abyssinia in Africa has a feathered face but wears an unfeathered dangling growth below its chin. It eats mice as well as snakes, frogs, and insects, and it nests in bushes growing out of cliffs along the rivers. Each bird of a flock of 50 to 100 wattled ibises, as they take flight together, gives one loud harsh call. With that roar they take off into the air.

The SACRED IBIS lives over most of Africa, but in Egypt where it got its name, it has been extinct for more than 100 years. In the tall papyrus along the Nile where Pharaoh's daughter found the baby Moses, the sacred ibis formerly hid its flimsy stick nest. It held 2 or 3 downy chicks that could swim when they tumbled into the water. They were fed on fish, frogs, snakes, and insects, especially locusts. Papyrus has long since vanished from the banks of the Nile and the sacred ibis with it. The only sacred ibises in Egypt today are those preserved in the tombs of the Pharaohs and in many ancient drawings and sculptures. In its present range the sacred ibis nests in various rushes as it did long ago, but also on flat-topped thorn trees, on rocky islets, and sometimes on trees in the villages.

The ibis family includes flat-billed birds that are called spoonbills.
See also: SPOONBILLS

Glossy Ibis

White Ibis

Scarlet Ibis

Sacred Ibis

American Jaçana

African Jaçana

Jaçanas
(Pronounced
Zā sā nā′)

On the marshy edges of lakes and rivers in the tropic lands of the world, the jaçanas walk across the water on floating water lily leaves. Their very long toes and long toenails stretch across several lily leaves each time the birds put a foot down. Their feet keep them from sinking into the water just as skis keep the skiers from sinking into the snow. Jaçanas wear a thornlike spur on the bend of each wing. It is a weapon with which they defend themselves.

Jaçanas swim well and dive to escape danger instead of flying from it. Their flight is usually slow, heavy, and low, but they can fly upward and circle. In spring the females grow courting plumes and court the males. The nests, made of water weeds and rubbish, float in quiet bays. In this odd family of 8 species the male birds incubate the 3 to 6 eggs for 3 weeks and raise the chicks. Jaçana chicks are downy when hatched and have long toes and nails. They soon can follow their male parent over the lily pads to hunt for insects, snails, fish and the seeds of water plants.

The 10-inch-long AMERICAN JAÇANA lives in Central America. It often crosses the border into southern Texas. The COMB-CRESTED JAÇANA lives in Borneo, Malaya, New Guinea, Australia and the Philippines. Its eggs shine as though they had been varnished.

Gray-headed Junco

Oregon Junco

White-winged Junco

Jays
See Crows

Juncos

These small sparrows have pink bills, dark hoods and bibs, white underparts, and a perky way of hopping on the ground. The SLATE-COLORED JUNCO breeds across Canada and south into the Appalachian Mountains. It winters throughout all but the southernmost of the United States. Four other kinds, the WHITE-WINGED JUNCO, the OREGON JUNCO, the GRAY-HEADED JUNCO, and the MEXICAN JUNCO, breed each in a different part of the high Rocky Mountains in spruce, fir, pine, and pin oak forests. They winter in the valleys and plains nearby, going from high ground to low.
See also: SPARROWS AND RELATED BIRDS

Killdeer

See Plovers

Kingbirds

See Flycatchers

Belted Kingfisher ♂

Malachite Kingfisher ♂

White-collared Kingfisher

Kingfishers

These birds avoid the icy regions of the world but are otherwise widespread. The 84 species are divided into those kingfishers that fish and those that do not. The 6 New World kingfishers all fish. They sit on a perch watching the water below them and dive into it to catch their prey. When swallowing a fish, kingfishers always turn the catch around with their bills so it goes down their throats head first. The scales and fin spines of a fish swallowed tail first would scratch their throats. When a kingfisher gets a fish too big to swallow it swallows the head and sits with the tail hanging out of its mouth, patiently waiting for the front end to digest and make room for the rest.

The BELTED KINGFISHER, the only kingfisher native to Alaska, Canada and the United States, is commonly seen perched above streams, ditches, and salt-water inlets along highways. The belted kingfisher migrates from the colder parts of its range to spend the winter where ice will not spoil its fishing. Its range extends into Central and South America where it shares the rivers with the toy-like PYGMY KINGFISHER, a minnow catcher.

Kingfishers are from 4 to 18 inches long; the belted is 13 inches and the pygmy only $5\frac{1}{4}$ inches. The largest in the New World is the 16-inch RINGED KINGFISHER found all the way from Mexico to Patagonia. The 7-inch GREEN KINGFISHER on rare occasions wanders from Mexico into southern Texas and Arizona, but lives regularly as far south as Peru.

Europe has only one kingfisher, the $6\frac{1}{2}$-inch COMMON KINGFISHER. Its habits and behavior are like those of the American belted kingfisher. The only kingfisher in Siberia, it, too, moves from the colder parts of its range in winter.

From central Asia to Australia and the Pacific islands and through Africa are scattered 77 more species of kingfishers. Outstanding among them is the big 15-inch black-and-white PIED KINGFISHER of southeast Asia. It lives along mountain streams where it catches fish and crayfish and comes down to lower valleys only when the streams freeze. After each catch it flies away with its prey in its mouth uttering its silver-toned call.

The WHITE-COLLARED KINGFISHER of southern Asia, Africa, Australia and many Pacific islands was a favorite of Chinese jewelers, who used its brilliant blue feathers like gems. White-collared kingfishers are forest kingfishers and do not fish. They eat lizards, tree frogs, beetles, bees, snakes, and grasshoppers. To kill the larger of its prey, the bird holds the animal in its bill and beats it against a branch.

The MALACHITE KINGFISHER of Africa, south of the Sahara Desert, is famed for its beauty, its swift flight, and its habit of raising and lowering its amazing crest. It fishes in lakes and the broad waters of the upper Nile.

The 17-inch LAUGHING KOOKABURRA or LAUGHING JACKASS KINGFISHER, of Australia, screams and laughs as it leaves its treetop roost at dawn and again at dusk when it returns. The equally large and much more colorful BLUE-WINGED KOOKABURRA turns the crazy laughter of the other kookaburra into whooping screams. These are forest kingfishers and a major part of their food is snakes and lizards. They kill this prey before swallowing it, often by dropping it onto a hard surface from high in the air.

The fishing kingfishers nest in a round cavity at the end of a 3- to 10-foot burrow in a steep river bank. Using their beaks as chisels and their feet as scoops, the mated pair work together to make a tunnel just big enough around to admit an adult bird. On the bare ground in the chamber at the end of the tunnel the female lays 2 clutches of 5 to 8 eggs a year. The eggs are incubated for from 18 to 24 days and the chicks are fed in the nest-hole for 3 to 4 weeks by their parents. The parents spend several days teaching the young how to fish after they leave the burrow before deserting them.

Forest kingfishers use holes in trees and in Africa drill burrows into the 10- and 12-foot-high termite colony mounds and also dig into bank and cliff sides to lay their eggs. The white-collared kingfisher and his mate chisel a hole in a tree with their strong bills by flying at one spot on the trunk at full speed from a perch 6 to 10 feet away. Each flight chips a bit of bark until the birds can get a toe hold and hammer at the wood. The kookaburras use natural cavities in trees as nest-holes.

The common kingfisher flies through the water just as it flies through the air and probably all the other fishing kingfishers do too.

Laughing Kookaburra

Kites

See Hawks

Kiwis

See Ostriches and Other Ratite Birds

Larks

Only one member of this family of 75 Old World songbirds is native to America. The HORNED LARK breeds throughout North America and Mexico except for western Alaska and the southeastern states. It migrates south from Canada in winter but can be seen the year around through the rest of its range. Like all larks it is a bird of meadows and large fields. It runs on the ground, never hops or perches on trees, but may alight on a fence post. Larks feed on weeds, seeds and insects. They lay 3 to 5 speckled eggs in a nest in a hollow in the ground or in the far north in mosses and lichens of the tundra.

The SKYLARK sings as it soars high into the air above its home meadows. It is native to Europe, Asia, and North Africa. Many skylarks have been brought to the

Skylark

Horned Lark

continental United States and released in the wild but none survived. It has been introduced successfully and is thriving on Vancouver Island in western Canada, in Hawaii, and in New Zealand.

American meadowlarks are not true larks but members of the blackbird family whose songs and habits reminded English settlers of European larks. EASTERN and WESTERN MEADOWLARKS look so much alike in the field that they can only be told apart by their very different songs.

See also: BLACKBIRDS

Limpkins

Limpkins are found in the swamps of South Carolina, Georgia, and Florida; also in Central America and southward to Argentina.

The limpkin is often called the "crying bird" from its 3 wailing notes that sound like the cries of a lost child on the marshes in the evening. The bird is much more often heard than seen. It is not shy, but just naturally finds its food in the far corners of the swamps. This is a pity because it is a most fascinating bird to watch. With a hesitating walk, as its name suggests, the limpkin limps over swamp muck hunting for apple snails. It stands about 2 feet high when erect, but walks with its head down, its powerful, slightly down-curved bill ready to probe for a snail and to pull it from its shell. When snails are scarce, limpkins will take crayfish, insects, and reptiles. At night they roost in trees.

Limpkins build a bulky nest of marsh plants in tall reeds or low trees and bushes near the water. It holds 6 splotched brown eggs which both parents incubate. No one knows exactly how long it takes for the young to hatch, but they are covered with down when they peck their way out of the shell. They can swim immediately. The parents and young birds remain together until the following spring.

Loons

Common Loon

Loons are the champion divers of the bird world. One was once caught in a fisherman's net set 240 feet below the surface. Loons are known to stay under water for as long as 5 minutes, but usually they make only shallow dives. They stay under water less than a minute, just long enough to catch a fish in their bills.

Loons are built for swimming and diving. They are shaped like torpedoes. Their leg bones are inside their bodies. Flat anklebones hold their webbed feet, like twin propellers, well behind their short, short tails. Their feet drive them through the water. With their wings they steer and balance under the water. For their weight loons have smaller wings than almost any other flying bird. Despite this they fly swiftly, reaching speeds up to 60 miles an hour. But they have trouble lifting themselves into the air. They have to spatter along the water, spanking it with their feet and flapping their wings wildly for as much as a quarter-mile before getting enough lift to take off.

On land loons are nearly helpless. Their propeller feet are not designed for walking, but sometimes they shove them against the ground to push themselves up and forward. They come down with a bump, having gained a little headway, and repeat the performance. Usually loons squirm forward on their breasts.

All 4 species of loons nest on freshwater lakes around the Arctic Circle, the ARCTIC LOON, the YELLOW-BILLED LOON and the RED-THROATED LOON, quite close to or within it. The COMMON LOON of the New World nests as far south as just below the Canadian border. The common loon and the red-throated loon spend the winter all along the Atlantic and Pacific Coasts of North America.

Loons do not build nests. The females lay 2 eggs in a hollow on the ground very close to water. While incubating both parent birds stretch out their necks and with their bills pull whatever is growing nearby around the eggs. As the eggs are incubated for a month, the downy black chicks may hatch on quite a pile of vegetation, but they leave it and take to the water with their parents almost at once. When the chicks get tired of swimming they scramble onto the parent's back for a ride. It takes them about 2 weeks to learn to dive and they are at least $2\frac{1}{2}$ months old before they try to fly.

Once heard, the calls of these birds linger in the memory forever. Their voices are loud and clear, and a wailing "ahaa-ooo-oooo-ooo-ooo-ahhh" echoes in the lake country of the north all during the summer months into the fall. At dusk, at night, and at dawn during the breeding months in early summer loons yodel a wild laughing song that resounds over the water. When loons flock in the fall they call each other together with a hoot so loud it can be heard more than a mile away. Loons are heard in the daytime when they have been disturbed by such noisy things as outboard motors.

Lyrebirds

Two species of these birds are found in the forests of eastern Australia. The male of the SUPERB LYREBIRD gave the family its name. When courting he throws his 16 tail plumes over his head. As they rise in the air they look exactly like the ancient Greek lyre, a harplike musical instrument. The plumes hold this pose for a second, then drop down in front of the bird, and he sings behind this curtain of feathers. His songs are varied and he practices new ones during the months when he is shedding his old tail and growing a new one. In addition to his own beautiful music, the male lyrebird can imitate the calls and songs of all the other birds in the forest, the voices of animals, and mechanical sounds such as motors and auto horns.

When a mated pair of lyrebirds choose an area as their own, they usually remain in it for life. The female builds a roofed nest on or near the ground with a side entrance. Her mate builds 2 or 3 mounds nearby. While she incubates her single egg he poses, dances, and sings on one or another of his mounds. While she feeds and broods the chick, he guards his family and entertains it.

Lyrebirds are the size of roosters and the longest perching birds in the world. Counting their 26-inch tails, the males measure 38 inches long, the females almost as much. ALBERT'S LYREBIRD does not have a lyre-shaped tail so it has not been painted as often as the superb.

Superb Lyrebird
♂

Magpies

See Crows

Martins

See Swallows

Brown Thrasher

Common Mockingbird

Catbird

Mockingbirds

To most Americans mockingbird means the 9-inch COMMON MOCKINGBIRD of every garden of the southern United States and Mexico. Actually mockingbirds are a New World family of 31 species of songsters with a wonderful way of adding to their own music the notes and calls of other birds. Their voices ring out from very early in spring until late in the fall, all day long and often under the light of the moon.

In the United States, in addition to the common mockingbird, the CATBIRD lives east of the Rocky Mountains, the BROWN THRASHER east of the Great Plains from southern Canada to the Gulf of Mexico, and the SAGE THRASHER west of the Mississippi from southern Canada into northern Mexico. The rest of the family live in Central America, the West Indies and South America. The southernmost is the PATAGONIAN MOCKINGBIRD of southern Argentina and Chile that lives on dry hills where there is little water. Like the common mockingbird, it also imitates the birds around it.

These "mimic birds" all have very similar habits. They do not go about in flocks. They live in pairs during the nesting season and alone the rest of the year. The male bird will not permit another male of the same species to come within the territory he considers his own. If his nest is in danger the common mockingbird will attack a cat or dog or even a man.

He flies out to peck his enemy's head. When he sees his reflection in a window he thinks he has found a rival and pecks at the glass. In a garden where they are protected, mockingbirds will become so tame that they will steal cookies from a tea tray only a few feet away from the tea drinkers. The common mockingbird has been called "the king of song," the "matchless mimic" and the "most beloved bird of the South."

The catbirds' mewing cry, very much like a cat's, gave these birds their name. Catbirds are at home some part of the year from southern Canada through most of the United States, except for California, Nevada, and the areas bordering on Mexico.

The ground-loving thrashers have longer tails than other mimics. They are more retiring but will scratch under the shrubbery and use the birdbath quite near the people they see daily. The brown thrasher is the brightest feathered of the family in the United States. It is not really brown but the ruddy shade of auburn hair. It is often found in the brush and shrubbery at the edge of pecan orchards. All the mimics build rather bulky nests of twigs, grasses, rootlets, bits of string and yarn, paper, hair, and bark in bushes and shrubs. In the cotton-growing states the common mockingbird often weaves a bit of cotton into its nest. On rare occasions the catbird and, more often, the brown thrasher put their nests on the ground, but 3 to 10 feet above it is the usual place for a mimic's nest. Male and female build together for the 2 to 5 blue or green eggs, usually speckled and about 1 inch long, that the female lays.

The mimic birds eat insects, fruit, and seeds, and feed their young on insects. All mockingbirds and the catbird will come to bird feeders for cut apples and oranges, for currants and raisins, and for bread cubes. They are also fond of peanut butter.

Murres

See Auks

Muttonbirds

See Petrels

Mynas

See Starlings

Nene

See Waterfowl

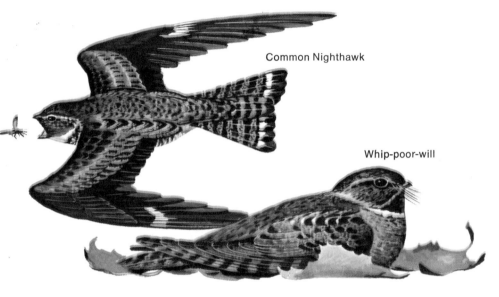

Common Nighthawk

Whip-poor-will

Nightjars

These birds are well named because their loud, repeated calls jar the ears of their neighbors during the warm nights of the year. CHUCK-WILL'S-WIDOW calls its name in southeastern United States and Central America, a low "chuck" and a clear "will's-wid-o." It has repeated the call as many as 834 times in succession on a June night as counted in a garden in Charleston, South Carolina.

The WHIP-POOR-WILL sings its name in eastern North America, the mountains of Arizona and New Mexico, and into Central America. It can repeat the "whip-poor-will" 100 times and more without pausing for breath. The POOR-WILL calls in western North America and Mexico. Its voice is harsh and sad. It says "poor-will-ee" but the "ee" is

very soft and can only be heard for a short distance.

The NIGHTHAWK isn't a hawk at all but a nightjar. It breeds throughout temperate North America and winters in South America from Columbia to Argentina. If it had been named for its call, it would be called the "buzzing-bird." Its cry is an insectlike buzz, but its flight is hawklike. As it flies before dark, it is seen more often than the other American nightjars. The COMMON NIGHT-JAR of Eurasia has a voice very similar to that of our nighthawk. It sounds more like a cricket than a bird, and it sometimes calls for 5 minutes at a time with no stop between its loud chirps.

The nighthawk often lays its 2 eggs on a flat roof in cities and towns. Other nightjars usually lay their 1 or 2 eggs on the bare ground.

Many people call the nightjars "goatsuckers." This name comes from the foolish, old belief that these birds used their wide mouths to milk goats. The Latin and scientific name of the family is *Caprimulgus* from *capra* meaning goat and *mulgus* meaning to milk.

Most nightjars are only 7 to 11 inches long, but the male STANDARD-WING NIGHTJAR of Africa grows 2 flaglike wing feathers in spring that are 2 feet long. The male LYRE-TAILED NIGHTJAR of the American tropics has 27-inch tail feathers to display to his mate.

The 67 nightjars all look very much alike, with brownish-grayish feathers and small white markings. The birds are invisible against bark and blend perfectly with dead leaves on the ground. When they roost on a broad tree limb during the day to sleep, they squat along it, not across it as most birds do. This is an unusual position for a bird, but it makes

the nightjar invisible. It looks like just another lump of bark on the tree.

Their feathers are very soft, making it possible for them to fly silently and swoop down upon flying insects without a sound. Their gaping open mouths, surrounded by bristles, look larger than their heads and trap insects and moths better than a butterfly net. Nightjars have such very short legs and tiny feet they cannot walk. On the ground they squat or go forward in a hobbling creep.

Some of the nightjars have other peculiar habits. Poor-wills very often hibernate during the winter instead of migrating. They crawl into cracks in the rocks and go to sleep. Their body temperature gets low, their heartbeat slows down, and their digestive system stops working. When spring arrives they come to life again.

Nuthatches

In the forests of North America, Eurasia, and Australia these small, 3½- to 7-inch acrobats walk up, down, and around tree trunks, always head first. Their name was originally "nuthackers" in England, where the EURASIAN NUTHATCH pushes nuts and acorns into cracks in trees while it hacks them open with its strong bill.

In North America the wide-ranging WHITE-BREASTED and RED-BREASTED NUTHATCHES do not eat many nuts or acorns. They live mainly on insects and insect eggs they find under tree bark. The red-breasted nuthatch eats a great many pine seeds and prefers pine forests to hardwoods. In the southeastern United States the BROWN-HEADED NUTHATCH lives in the southern pines. In western states, the 3½-inch PYGMY NUTHATCH lives in woodlands up to 10,000 feet above sea level.

The nuthatches of Eurasia and North America use holes in trees and rock crevices, lined with bits of bark, grass

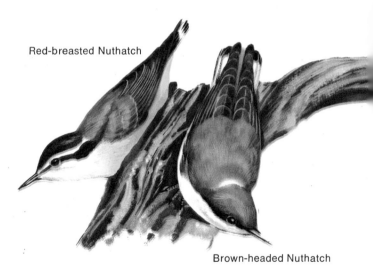

Red-breasted Nuthatch

Brown-headed Nuthatch

and twigs, to hold their 4 to 12 red-spotted white eggs. Sometimes nuthatches peck out their own holes. The white-breasted and red-breasted nuthatches occasionally nest in bird boxes. The eggs are incubated for about 2 weeks, usually by both parents. The young birds leave the nest-holes before they can fly. They crawl about on nearby branches where they also roost at night. The parents feed them until they can fly.

In Australia the nuthatches are known as sittellas from their Latin name *Sittidae*. The BLACK-CAPPED SITTELLA and WHITE-CAPPED SITTELLA are brightly patterned birds of open forests. They behave like the American and European nuthatches but have different nesting habits. They weave nests of spider webs, cocoons, and bark that look so like the branches they are fastened to that they are hard to see. Each pair of sittellas raises only 3 chicks each year.

Orioles

See Blackbirds

Ospreys

Osprey

The osprey is a big fish-eating bird of prey, 24 inches long, related to falcons and hawks, but placed in a family of its own. It lives near lakes, rivers, and oceans on all the large land masses of the world. The ospreys that breed in North and Central America winter in South America. Those that breed in Eurasia winter in Africa. The ospreys that breed in Australia stay there the year round.

Ospreys catch fish by plunging into the water, feet first, with half-closed wings from high in the air. They grab the fish with both feet and carry it, head first, to the nest or to a perch. Ospreys are often annoyed at their fishing grounds by bald eagles and frigate-birds that force them to drop their fish. In turn the ospreys drive all hawks and falcons away from their nesting area. In this way, ospreys protect smaller birds around them and even the farmers' poultry. Any farmer is lucky to have an osprey nest in his yard.

Ospreys have very dainty eating habits. They take small bites of their fish, tearing pieces off with their beaks. After eating they return to the water and splash into the surface to clean their feet, feathers, and beaks.

In America ospreys build their large bulky nests on top of trees and telephone poles. The nest is repaired and used year after year, for as long as 40 years. Each spring the female lays 3 white eggs spattered with red and brown which she incubates for 5 weeks with some help from her mate. The chicks remain in the nest for 8 to 10 weeks. The mother feeds them with fish that the father brings to her at the nest.

Ostriches and Other Ratite Birds

The breastbones of most birds are shaped like the keel of a boat. They stick out like the breastbone of the turkey from which the white meat is carved on Thanksgiving Day. The bird's flying muscles are attached to this keel-shaped bone. When land birds that do not exercise their wings become flightless over a period of millions of years, they lose their flying muscles. Then gradually their breastbones flatten out and look like rafts instead of keels. The Latin word for raft is *ratis* and from it comes the word "ratite." It is used to describe a number of large flightless extinct birds and 5 families of flightless living birds.

The kiwis of New Zealand are the smallest living ratites, about as big as good-sized chickens. The NORTH ISLAND KIWI, the STEWART ISLAND KIWI and the GRAY KIWI all look so much alike that only an expert can tell them apart. The first two are reddish gray and the third is brownish gray. Their feathers look much like hair. They have no tails and their wings are only 2 inches long and hidden under the body feathers. Their nostrils are at the tip of their long 6-inch bills, and they probably smell their way around because they cannot see well.

Kiwis spend the day in the burrows they dig under tree roots and into banks of forest ridges. They spend the night pushing their long bills into the soft ground for grubs and worms. The female kiwi lays an egg 5 inches long, almost one fourth of her own length, and it weighs almost a pound. It is incubated by the male for about 2 months. The kiwi chick is ready to follow its parents into the swampy forest soon after it hatches. Years ago the Maoris of New Zealand made feather cloaks of kiwi skins.

The largest living ratites are: the OSTRICH, a family of 1 species found in southern Africa; the EMU, a family of 1 species in Australia; the cassowaries— the AUSTRALIAN CASSOWARY in Australia and New Guinea, and BENNETT'S CASSOWARY and the ONE-WATTLED CASSOWARY both found only in New Guinea; the rheas—the COMMON RHEA in Brazil, Uruguay, and Argentina, and DARWIN'S RHEA from southern Peru to the Straits of Magellan.

These are the largest birds in the world. The ostrich stands 8 feet tall and weighs up to 345 pounds. The emu is $5\frac{1}{2}$ feet

Common Rhea

Ostrich

Bennett's Cassowary

Emu

Gray Kiwi

tall and weighs up to 120 pounds. The Australian cassowary is $5\frac{1}{2}$ feet tall and up to 74 pounds; the Bennett's cassowary about a foot shorter and 15 pounds lighter. The common rhea stands the same height but is 10 pounds lighter and the Darwin's rhea is $3\frac{1}{2}$ feet tall and weighs up to 35 pounds.

All 4 families have very similar ways, although they live far from one another. They all eat juicy plants, berries, seeds, fruits, and also any insects they find. They all wear colors that make them practically invisible to an enemy in the distance when they crouch against the ground. The ostrich in the desert hides this way, so the silly story was told that ostriches hide by sticking their heads in the sand. The big ratites escape from their enemies by running. Some can reach a speed of 40 miles an hour. The common rhea always lifts one of its small wings as though raising a sail when it runs. They all can escape enemies by swimming, even the ostrich whose desert home does not offer many swimming holes.

When cornered the big ratites fight by kicking out and down with their long powerful legs or by jumping feet first at an enemy. The claw on the larger of the ostrich's 2 toes and the claws on the others' 3 toes are so strong they will gash and tear a lion or a man.

When it is near the right time of year for breeding, the males of the big ratites send booming calls echoing over the countryside. They sound much like a lion's roar but are pleasing to the 3 to 6 hens in the male's harem. The male pre-

pares a scrape on the ground and his hens may lay 10 to 40 eggs in it. The ostrich's favorite mate shares the work of incubating the eggs and raising the chicks. The other ratite males do it alone. The chicks are born with short legs and covered with down. A few hours after hatching they are ready to join the family group.

An ostrich egg is white, nearly round, as big as a baby's head, and has a thick pitted shell. Its contents are equal to between 2 and $2\frac{1}{2}$ dozen chicken eggs. It will serve 12 to 15 people when scrambled.

An emu egg and an Australian cassowary egg are both dark green, oval, and have pitted shells that are rubbed glossy during incubation. The contents of either of them is equal to a dozen medium chicken eggs.

A common rhea egg is greenish tan with a rough thick shell, and is about 5 inches long. Its contents are equal to about 8 large chicken eggs.

African Bushmen blow the contents out of ostrich eggs through a small hole and use the shell as a water bottle. Emu eggs contain so much oil that the cook must skim it off before using the egg.

Ostriches, rheas, cassowaries and the emu were all much more plentiful in the past than they are today. Ostriches were taken for their plumes, leather, and meat. Ostrich-feather fans were so popular at one time that birds were raised on ostrich farms in Florida and California and plucked regularly. Common rheas are taken for meat and to make feather dusters. Both species of cassowary are food for the natives of New Guinea. The emu is taken for meat and killed because it damages the crops. The kiwis' enemies are the dogs and cats settlers have brought to New Zealand.

In addition to the ratites more than 40 different kinds of living birds no longer fly. They use their wings for balancing or swimming and have not lost the keel on their breastbones.

Burrowing Owl

Snowy Owl

World-wide land birds, the owls are separated into 2 families, the barn owls with 9 species, and typical owls with 123 species. There are family likenesses between the 2 groups, but also differences. Barn owls' small eyes look out of heart-shaped faces over rather long, hooked beaks. Typical owls' very large eyes look out of round faces over short, hooked beaks. Barn owls' longish legs are feathered but their toes are bare. On 1 toe of each foot the claw is a toothed comb with which the birds preen their feathers. Typical owls' very short legs and toes are feathered. Both have soft plumage, but barn owls' body feathers are shorter than those of typical owls.

Barn owls' screams are shrill and scary. They also chuckle, snore and hiss. Typical owls hoot, trill, bark, whistle, and snap their bills with a click like snapping fingers. The 8-inch-long SCREECH OWL does not really screech but whistles sadly with trembling, falling notes. The screech owl, like many typical owls, wears earlike tufts of feathers on its head that barn owls do not grow. It is found in the United States, the west coast of Canada, and in northern Mexico.

Owls cannot move their eyeballs. They always look in the direction their head faces and their limber necks make it possible for them to turn their heads a complete half-circle to look straight behind themselves.

Barn owls are from 13 to 18 inches long, typical owls from $5\frac{1}{4}$ to 27 inches long. All female owls are a few inches longer than their mates. All owls eat and hunt in the same way, most of them hunt at night. They catch small mammals, birds, reptiles, amphibians, fish, crabs, and insects. Owls find their prey more by listening than looking. When its prey is found the owl swoops down swiftly and silently to grab the creature in its claws. It swallows the prey whole and later on coughs out neat little balls, called pellets, of fur, bone, feathers, and other parts it cannot digest.

In mild climates barn owls have no

regular breeding time. A pair, mated for life, raise young when food is plentiful. All barn owls have very similar breeding habits.

The COMMON BARN OWL is the only barn owl found in the New World. It makes itself useful to man by eating mice and rats from southern Canada to the southern tip of South America and in parts of Eurasia, Africa, and Australia. In California it also eats ground squirrels and gophers. At any time of the year when these rodents are in good supply a pair of common barn owls hunt a breeding place, or return to their old one. It may be a barn loft, a church steeple, a cave, a hollow tree, an empty building, a tunnel, or even another animal's old burrow in the ground. Without making a nest, the female lays from 5 to 11 round white eggs, 1 every 2 or 3 days, in the chosen hole. Both parents incubate the eggs, sometimes cosily sitting on them together. At the end of 24 days the first-laid egg hatches. The others follow in the order in which they were laid. So the first chick hatched will be at least 2 weeks old when the seventh chick pecks its way out of its shell. Each chick remains in the nest until it is 2

months old. A half-grown chick eats as many as 8 mice a night, and says it is hungry by making a sound like soup being sucked noisily.

Barn owls do not migrate but some typical owls do. The PUEO, a typical owl in Hawaii and another mouse eater, moves around the islands to where mice are most plentiful. Long ago Hawaiians worshiped this owl as a god.

The SNOWY OWL is a true migrant. It nests on the ground on the arctic tundras the world around and comes as far south in winter as the Great Lakes in this hemisphere and France and Siberia in Eurasia. It hunts by day, its white feathers camouflaging it against the snow. One of the first bird pictures ever drawn is of a pair of snowy owls with their chick scratched on the wall of a cave in France by a Stone Age man.

Common in both Americas is the GREAT HORNED OWL that likes to raise its 2 to 5 young in the old nests of red-tailed hawks or bald eagles, as well as in caves and hollow trees. It sometimes eats the common barn owl.

East of the Rocky Mountains in the United States and southern Canada the 17-inch-long BARRED OWL is often seen

Barn Owl

Elf Owl

during the day, although it is a night-hunter. It is sometimes caught far from home at daylight. Then as it sits dozing it may be found by crows who will scold and tease it until it leaves in distress. This owl raises 2 or 3 young each spring and feeds them all summer and fall, long after they can fly.

The 8-inch BURROWING OWL found west of the Mississippi and in Florida digs its own burrows 1 to 3 feet under the ground. The pair take turns incubating their 5 to 7 eggs and always bow to each other when they meet before their entrance hole. Many nest between the runways at the Miami airport in Florida, paying no attention to the great jet planes roaring by.

The smallest owl in the world is the 5¼-inch ELF OWL of the deserts of southwestern United States and northern Mexico. It rests by day in holes in giant cactus and nests in them, too, raising 3 chicks a year on an insect diet.

Oystercatchers

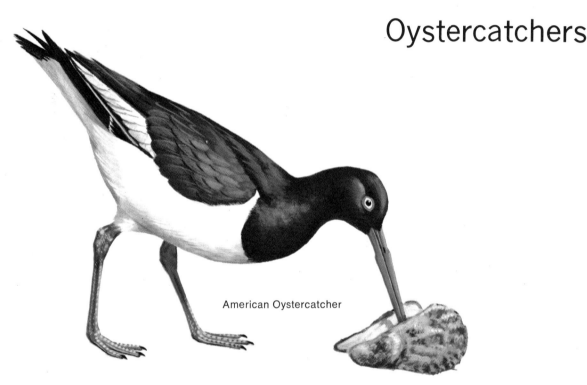

American Oystercatcher

These shy but showy wading birds are found on seacoasts where the climate is mild on all continents, and on inland waters in the Old World. Most notable in any of the six kinds of oystercatchers is its strong bill, 2 times longer than its head. The bill is used like a chisel to pry clinging shells from rocks. It is used as a probe to find insects and shellfish in the sand. It is used like a hammer to pound clams and mussels on the shore until the shells break. Like a pair of pincers, it snatches a living oyster from its half-open shell.

The AMERICAN OYSTERCATCHER lays its 2 or 3 eggs in dry mud or sand above the high tide line in spring. Both parents in turn incubate the eggs when the sun is very hot to keep them from cooking and in the cool of night to keep them from chilling. The chicks hatch in about 3 weeks and run about immediately.

Male EUROPEAN OYSTERCATCHERS compete with each other in a courtship dance for a watching female. When she finally picks the male she likes, she remains mated to him for several years. One European oystercatcher banded as a nestling returned to the place it was hatched 36 years later.

Parrots

People of North America, Europe, and northern Asia are apt to think of parrots as bright-colored talking birds in cages in zoos, pet shops, and private homes. Actually, in the tropical and subtropical countries they come from, they are heard and seen as often as crows are here. Like crows, they fly screaming through the woodlands and they raid orchards and grain fields in flocks. They eat fruit, nuts, grain, plant leaves, flowers, and nectar. When eating they usually perch on one foot and use the other to lift the fruit or spike of grain to their beaks.

Most parrots lay their 1 to 12 round white eggs in bare holes in trees. The 3½-inch rainbow-colored PYGMY PARROT of the Solomon Islands lays in a hollow dead limb and the LESSER PYGMY PARROT of New Guinea lays in a hole it digs in a termite nest with live termites for neighbors. The GRAY-BREASTED PARAKEET, also called monk or Quaker parakeet, of South America builds a nest of sticks and twigs so large it would overload a pick-up truck. In it many pairs each have their own private room.

The large long-tailed gaudy MACAWS of tropical America are favorites of zoo keepers. Although they never learn to say more than a word or two and scream shrilly, they are healthy in captivity, become very tame, and may live 50 years or more.

The best talkers in the New World, the 20-inch-long Amazon parrots native to South and Central America become affectionate pets. The YELLOW-HEADED AMAZON of Mexico is a favorite, but parrot fanciers claim the AFRICAN GRAY PARROT is the best talker in the world. When parrots learn to speak they just mimic sounds without understanding what they mean. If a parrot says something sensible, it is entirely by accident.

From Africa, Madagascar, and southern Asia come parrots that do not learn to

Blue and Yellow Macaw

Kaka

Yellow-headed Amazon

Painted Lorikeet

speak, but perch for hours bill to bill as though in love with one another. The ROSY-FACED LOVEBIRD is a favorite in the United States. Pet-shop dealers call it the PEACH-FACED LOVEBIRD. A pair often build a nest and raise young in their cage.

Australia and Malaya are the home of many parrots. Lories and lorikeets fly in huge flocks. As many as 1,000 RAINBOW LORIKEETS are seen at one time, moving and alighting together as they look for flowers to crush in their bills. Cockatoo flocks live on ripening grain and orchard fruit. The BLACK COCKATOO of New Guinea with its large bill cracks nuts that a man would use a hammer on. BUDGERIGARS, most plentiful birds in Australia, are black and yellow above and green below in the wild. Breeders have changed the colors of these popular talking pets by mating the odd-colored birds that occasionally hatch out.

New Zealand is home to some of the oddest parrots in the world. The KAKAPO or OWL PARROT that has lost the power to fly, runs and climbs during the night. The birds scream, and during the breeding season which occurs in spring every other year, the males boom like primitive drums. The green, brown, and crimson KAKA once provided meat and feathered capes to the native Maori people and came to settlers' homes in huge flocks shrieking and whistling. It was declared a pest and now only a few survive in scattered forests. The KEA lives on flowers and nectar on the mountains in summer. In the winter snow drives it to the valleys for food. Here it has come to like mutton. It eats dead sheep and may even attack live ones. It is the only meat-eater among the parrots.

Extinct parrots include the CAROLINA PARAKEET of North America. It roamed the eastern forests as far west as Colorado and from Lake Erie south to Texas and Florida. By 1889 only a few small flocks were left in Oklahoma and in Florida. The last Carolina parakeet shot in the wild was taken in Florida in 1904. It is now in the American Museum of Natural History in New York.

Black Cockatoo

Budgerigar

Kea

Partridges

See Pheasants

Peafowl

See Pheasants

Pelicans

Pelicans lived in the warmer waters of the world about 35 million years ago, just as they do today. During the centuries since then, pelicans have remained almost unchanged. Scientists tell us the bones of the 6 species living now are much like those of fossil pelicans. Probably their appearance and habits also resemble those of their ancestors.

A pelican stands and lurches along on webbed feet with which he can perch on a tree or swim in the sea. From his stout straight long bill hangs a leathery, unfeathered pouch. This pouch is a dip net with which the bird fishes and also a feeding bowl for its chicks. A pelican never carries fish in its pouch. When it has caught a pouchful of fish the bird tips its bill forward to let the water run out of pouch and bill, and then throws its head back and swallows the catch. If it is feeding young birds, it returns to its nest, coughs the half-digested fish back into the pouch, and dribbles a little of this fish chowder into the open bills of the youngest chicks. Older chicks put their heads into the parents' pouch and help themselves. When a pelican is not using its pouch, the bird pulls it in so it lies flat against the bill. A pelican at rest sits with its bill pointed down so its pouch is hidden. A flying pelican pulls its neck back and points its bill downward, again hiding the pouch.

All pelicans are sociable and like to be in each other's company. They fly, roost, feed, and breed in groups. In flight pelicans follow one another in a long line. Each repeats the movements of the first bird in the line in turn like children playing follow-the-leader. Pelicans are 4 to 6 feet long from the ends of their stubby tails to the tips of their long bills. Their wings when spread measure 6 feet for the smallest species to 10 feet for the biggest species. Pelicans fold their wings together like an accordion when they come to rest.

Pelicans float well because they have hollow bones that weigh little. From their lungs they inflate many air sacs, like little balloons, under their skin. Pelicans spread their webbed feet out as though to break their fall when they bounce into the water. They push against the water with their feet to rise into the air.

The BROWN PELICAN of the tropical and temperate American coasts fishes by diving into the water from the air and scooping up fish from the sea. The Seri Indians of California Bay used these pelicans as fishermen. They tied a living pelican to a stake near the shore and took the fish other pelicans brought to the captive bird.

One of the largest breeding colonies of this bird is Pelican Island in Florida, the first National Wildlife Refuge. The brown pelican's rough stick nests may be placed on the ground, in low bushes, or in mangrove trees. Each pair of brown pelicans raises 3 or 4 chicks that hatch from 3-inch-long white eggs.

Brown pelicans were once very plentiful in Louisiana, which is known as the "Pelican State." The brown pelicans are no longer found there. They died after eating fish poisoned by insect sprays that had seeped into the rivers and ponds.

Five species of pelicans are white. They nest on islands and shores of freshwater lakes in Africa, Eurasia, Australia, and western United States. A large colony of American WHITE PELICANS breed on Great Salt Lake in Utah. These birds migrate in winter to the coasts of southern United States and Mexico. They fish in a group. The birds form a half-circle facing the shore and with great splashing drive the fish toward the shore where they can easily be caught.

Brown Pelican

White Pelican

Penguins

King Penguin

Adelie Penguin

Most penguin pictures that Europeans and Americans see are of the 2 species that live and breed on the icy coasts of Antarctica. They are the great EMPEROR PENGUIN that stands 4 feet tall and weighs up to 100 pounds, and the small $2\frac{1}{2}$-foot-high ADELIE PENGUIN. As these birds always appear against a background of snow and ice, people are apt to think that all penguins live in Antarctica. Actually 13 other species of penguins live elsewhere in the Southern Hemisphere along coasts touched by cold water currents that flow northward from antarctic seas. One of these currents flows to within a few degrees of the equator, and there, on the Galapagos Islands not far from mainland South America, lives the GALAPAGOS PENGUIN. Other cold currents flow along the coasts of New Zealand, Australia, South Africa, and southern South America.

Penguins lost the ability to fly millions of years ago. Their wings have turned into flat, strong flippers with which they paddle themselves through and under the water. They steer themselves with their feet. Sometimes they swim like porpoises, going a few yards under water, then leaping forward a foot above the sea, breathing while in the air. They can travel about 15 miles an hour in this way. When they come ashore some can leap out of the water and land on their feet on a ledge or ice cake 10 to 12 feet above it.

Penguins' short legs and feet grow far back on their bodies, forcing them to stand upright. They waddle about looking like old-fashioned gentlemen in black cutaway coats and white shirts. Their flippers hanging at their sides look much more like human arms than bird wings. The ROCKHOPPER PENGUIN of New Zealand, Tasmania, the Falklands, and other southern islands is the most awkward of the penguins on land. It hops instead of walking, and it uses its bill and flippers to help it scramble up rocky cliffs. The

Adelie penguin is the most nimble but can run only as fast as a man can walk. Adelie penguins in a hurry flop down and go "belly-whopping" over the snow as fast as a man skis. The thick feathers that grow all over the birds cushion them as they slide along.

The emperor penguin mates and breeds in the coldest months of the antarctic winter. Each female lays a single egg and then goes back to the sea to feed, leaving her mate to incubate it alone. Holding the egg on top of his feet under a loose flap of belly skin, the male emperor stands or shuffles about on the ice. He goes without food for 64 long days of the antarctic night until the egg hatches. The chick is first fed penguin milk which forms in the male's crop during his long fast. When the female returns from the sea a few days later, she feeds the chick half-digested seafood from her crop. She looks after the chick for 2 or 3 weeks while the male goes to sea to eat. When the milder weather of antarctic summer arrives the chick is ready to go to sea. The KING PENGUIN, which lives on various islands at the edge of the Antarctic Circle, has similar breeding habits to the emperor, but the male and female kings take turns incubating about every 2 weeks.

All penguins nest in colonies. All but the king and emperor penguins incubate their 1 or 2 eggs by sitting over them on nests made of grass, sticks, or round stones. The nests may be on bare ground like those of the Adelie penguin, or in caves and burrows, and under rocks like the FAIRY PENGUINS' of Australia, or in thick vegetation like those of the YELLOW-EYED PENGUIN of New Zealand. The Galapagos penguin incubates its 2 eggs on the lava flow of an extinct volcano. Penguin colonies are very noisy. The birds bark, bray, trumpet, and croak at one another and at any intruder. They defend themselves and their young by hitting out with their flippers.

Emperor Penguin

Rockhopper Penguin

69

Manx Shearwater

Leach's Petrel

Petrels

Petrels are relatives of the albatrosses and like them are tube-nosed swimmers. In the family are also shearwaters and the FULMAR. Their Latin family name, *Procellariidae* (pronounced pro-cell-a-rī-ĕ-dē), means "of storms" or "of hurricanes." Closely related are 2 other families, the storm-petrels and the diving-petrels. All these birds have similar habits and are seen so often during stormy weather that crews of sailing vessels believed seeing them meant a storm was coming. Sailors today are still superstitious about petrels and their kin.

Birds of this group spend almost their entire lives flying over the sea riding the high winds on their long slender wings. The shearwaters swoop down into the watery valleys between the great waves, skimming or "shearing" the surface of the water on motionless wings. Others run and patter over the surface with fluttering wings. They are the petrels named for St. Peter who is said to have walked on water. Fulmar comes from an old Norse name meaning "foul gull" from its unpleasant musty smell.

These birds of the tempests dip food from the sea in flight or they swim on the surface to feed paddling with their webbed feet. They eat fish, squid, shell-fish, the fat and meat of dead whales and seals, and ships' garbage thrown overboard. In addition to using this food for growth and energy, the petrels and their kin make it into a musty-smelling, oily wax in their stomachs. This oil is shot out of a bird's mouth at an enemy. It is also dribbled out of the nose tubes and used to preen the plumage. It is passed from one bird to another in courtship and it is fed to newly-hatched chicks mixed with half-digested fish.

All the birds of the tempest, wherever they may wander over the oceans of the world, return in spring each to its own nesting colony. These colonies sometimes number a half-million breeding pairs of birds. To birds of the far north spring comes in May; to those near the Antarctic in November.

After a week or so of courting in neighboring seas, each pair picks a nesting place. The fulmars use rock ledges on cliffs hanging over the sea. The shearwaters and petrels dig burrows on the heights of rugged ocean islands. Each pair incubates a single large white egg for about $1\frac{1}{2}$ to 2 months, male and female taking turns. They stay with the chick during its first week of life and then return to sea. For the 6 to 14 weeks

Fulmar

that the chick remains in the colony, the parents come to it only to bring food. Just before it can fly they desert it. The young bird makes its way to the sea alone.

Common off the Atlantic Coast of North America from May to September is the GREATER SHEARWATER. It breeds in the Tristan da Cuñha Islands in the far South Atlantic during their spring and summer months, November, December, and January.

The SLENDER-BILLED SHEARWATER breeds on Australian islands and the Australians call it the MUTTONBIRD. It migrates in a great circle in the Pacific Ocean. It flies north past the Philippines, along the coast of Japan toward Alaska, and then southward past the west coast of North America, across the equator, and back to its breeding islands. Each year when the muttonbird chicks are the fattest, just before the parents desert them, the Australians harvest thousands of them. They are canned and sold as "Tasmanian squab." The oil is drained from them so they do not taste fishy.

Most common of the petrels in the North Atlantic and North Pacific is LEACH'S PETREL. WILSON'S PETREL is often seen following ships in the North Atlantic during the summer months. It returns to Antarctica to breed each November. These birds are not much bigger than the American robin, but their wing spread is twice their own length. Most petrels and shearwaters are small, but the GIANT PETREL of antarctic islands and southern oceans, is 36 inches long.

The fulmar is 19 inches long. In the Northern Hemisphere it nests at the edge of the Arctic Circle. In the Southern Hemisphere the SILVER-GRAY FULMAR nests at the edge of the Antarctic Circle. The fulmar is the only bird that has supported an entire community. The people of the Islands of St. Kilda off Scotland lived on fulmars for several centuries. They ate fulmar chicks and salted them for winter use. They burned fulmar oil in their lamps. They ate fulmar eggs cooked in fulmar fat and they slept on and under fulmar feathers and down. The last St. Kildan left the islands in 1930 and the 30,000 fulmars there are now increasing and spreading to other British islands. The Islands of St. Kilda are now a wildlife refuge, managed and protected by the British Nature Conservancy.

See also: ALBATROSSES

Phalaropes

Red Phalarope ♀

Northern Phalarope ♀

Wilson's Phalarope ♀

The 3 species of phalaropes are shore birds that have adapted themselves to life on the water. Instead of running along the beaches to feed like sandpipers, they paddle on the surface of the water with partly webbed feet. Bobbing their heads back and forth, they spin around in circles dipping up animal food with their bills.

Female phalaropes are larger than males and wear brighter feathers. On the breeding grounds in the far north, they do all the courting and let the males build the grass and moss nests. After laying 4 black- and brown-speckled tan eggs the females leave for the nearby ponds while the male birds incubate the eggs and raise the chicks.

The RED PHALAROPE and the NORTHERN PHALAROPE breed on arctic and subarctic tundras in North America and Eurasia and migrate over the oceans to winter in the Atlantic and Pacific. WILSON'S PHALAROPE migrates from the northern prairies of North America to winter on South American inland waters.

Pheasants

Although they look very different from one another, the magnificent male pheasant, the gaudy peafowl, the barnyard rooster, the quail (the smallest member of the family), and the partridge all have a common ancestor and belong to the same family. They are ground birds that scratch with their feet and probe with their bills for insects and worms. They also eat grain, seeds, acorns, buds, and berries. They have 4-toed, bare feet and stout, strong legs. The males of most species have a spur above the hind toe that is used as a weapon.

Quails, never more than 9 inches long, and partridges have short tails. Pheasants and jungle fowl have long tails. Peacocks have very long ornamental feathers just above their short tails. When these feathers are spread out and displayed, the cock looks as though he is carrying an enormous fan behind himself.

The pheasant family are all heavy birds with rounded wings. They can fly very fast for a short distance and are the hunters' ideal of a fine sporting target. Only 1 species migrates, the EURASIAN QUAIL that flies to Africa in winter. All the others wander over the territory where they were hatched. They like trees to roost in at night and brush and bushes for cover.

The pheasant family nests on the ground except for the tragopans or

Bobwhite Quail
♂

California Quail
♂

Argus Pheasant
♂

Ring-necked Pheasant
♂

Golden Pheasant
♂

Hungarian Partridge
♂

horned pheasants of Asia. The CRIMSON-BELLIED TRAGOPAN has fleshy blue horns and blows up a bright blue pouch when courting his mottled brown mate. She and all the other horned pheasants build bulky nests in trees.

Quails and partridges scrape a hollow in the ground in thick bush or grainfields. A male and female together raise 12 to 18 chicks. They stay together in family groups, called coveys, until late fall.

Peacocks, jungle cocks, barnyard cocks, and pheasant cocks spread their long fancy feathers and raise their crests as they pose for the females. They crow and give harsh calls. The peacocks scream. Each male mates with a harem of 2 to 5 females and each female scrapes her own hollow nest hidden in long grass or shrubbery. The ARGUS PHEASANT and PEACOCK PHEASANT hens each raise only 2 chicks a year. Other kinds of pheasant hens raise 6 to 12 chicks, some as many as 20, in a brood.

The chicks of all the pheasant family hatch covered with down. In less than an hour the down dries and the fluffy chick is ready to follow the hen to scratch for its own worms and pick its own seeds and berries.

In the New World the only native members of the pheasant family are the American quails. The BOBWHITE QUAIL calls his name in spring east of the Great Plains from Maine south to Guatemala. CALIFORNIA QUAIL and MOUNTAIN QUAIL of the West Coast, and SCALED QUAIL and GAMBLE'S QUAIL of the Southwest are not musical. Their cries are crow-like. In Central and South America small brown wood quails represent the family. The MARBLED WOODQUAIL sings duets with its mate in spring.

Man has added to these North American birds the RING-NECKED PHEASANT from Asia. It is well established in the northern states. The HUNGARIAN PARTRIDGE from Eurasia is well established in the Middle West, and the European ROCK PARTRIDGE in the Far West.

The native home of the most beautiful members of the family, the peafowls, the jungle fowls, and the pheasants, is central and southern Asia. From there they have been carried all over the world. Centuries ago the Romans brought ring-necked pheasants to Europe where they are now at home in the wild. Other pheasants were brought to zoos and aviaries. Pheasants can be bred away from their native homes more easily than almost any other game birds.

The first GOLDEN PHEASANTS were brought to Europe in 1740. From there Lafayette sent a pair to George Washington, who kept them in his garden at Mount Vernon. The SILVER PHEASANT appeared in Chinese poetry 5,000 years ago. One of the most colorful pheasants was found in the mountains of China in 1828 by Lord Amherst. He named it for his wife. LADY AMHERST PHEASANTS, released in an English park many years ago, have bred and multiplied as happily as though still in their native mountains.

The GREEN PHEASANT, national bird of Japan, is believed by the Japanese to foretell earthquakes.

The national bird of Ceylon is the CEYLON JUNGLE FOWL. The RED JUNGLE FOWL, alive in Asia now, was domesticated more than 3,200 years ago and is the ancestor of all barnyard chickens.

The GREEN PEAFOWL is the national bird of Burma. Until recently it was thought that all peafowls came from Asia. But in 1930 American explorers discovered the CONGO PEAFOWL in the wet jungles in Africa.

In Australia the AUSTRALIAN QUAIL is native, and was also in New Zealand until 1869. Netted by native Maoris and hunted by settlers, this quail did not survive when great brush fires destroyed its food and bushy cover. The ring-necked pheasant introduced to New Zealand in the 19th century met much the same fate.

See also: CHICKENS; DOMESTIC BIRDS; GALLINACEOUS BIRDS; TURKEYS

Jambu Fruit Dove

Mourning Dove

Bleeding Heart Pigeon

English has 2 names for these gentle cooing birds—the Anglo-Saxon word "dove" and the French word "pigeon." The family name is pigeon and it is also used for those kinds that are over a foot long and heavy. "Dove" is generally used for the smaller of the family's 289 species.

Some kind of pigeon occurs in every part of the world where fruits, seeds, grains, or acorns grow. The pigeons of the North Temperate Zone are from 6 to 16 inches long, but some of the tropical kinds are very large. The CROWNED PIGEON of New Guinea is as long as a bald eagle, 33 inches. Pigeons all have small heads on rather short, thick necks, and a spot of bare skin above their bills. They like to bathe in sun and in water, but they do not swim. They can suck water up and drink without tipping their heads back to let it roll down their throats as most other birds have to do. Pigeons sway as they walk on their short legs and they cling to a perch with their grasping toes. They fly strongly and many northern species migrate.

Wherever pigeons nest, in trees, on rock ledges, on buildings, or on the ground, they build flimsy platforms of sticks to hold their 1 to 3 eggs. Both parents feed the newly hatched squabs "pigeon milk." This is formed from the lining of each parent's crop, which flakes off. Pigeon milk looks very much like cheese and, like cheese, is rich in protein and fats. When the squabs are able to fly, the parents desert them. Domestic pigeons raise 3 or more broods a year. Other pigeons raise 1 or 2 in the north, 2 or 3 farther south.

The commonest pigeons in the world are the ROCK PIGEONS, originally found in Eurasia and Africa. These are the pigeons Noah is supposed to have had on the Ark. The first rock pigeons tamed were the ancestors of all domestic pigeons. Many domestic pigeons have escaped and live in freedom in the cities. In the wild they breed on rock cliffs and ledges. In the cities they breed on skyscraper ledges and house eaves and perch on statues in public parks. In the wild they eat as other pigeons do. In cities they live on handouts of stale bread, popcorn, crackerjacks, scraps, and garbage. In the far north and Antarctica, the rock pigeons cannot survive, but everywhere else Europeans have carried the rock pigeon with them. Spanish and Portuguese brought it to South America, Englishmen to New Zealand and Australia, and everyone to North America.

The commonest wild pigeon in North and Central America is the 10-inch-long MOURNING DOVE. Its sad, mournful cooing gives the bird its name. Mourning doves are protected in Canada and most of the northern United States, but they are shot as game birds in the southern states.

The PASSENGER PIGEON of North America and the FLOCK PIGEON of Australia (also called the HARLEQUIN BRONZE-WING) have had similar histories. When early European settlers arrived on these continents they found each of these pigeons in great numbers. The passenger pigeons followed ripening fruit through the country east of the Great Plains from Quebec to Florida, and the flock pigeon followed ripening grains and grasses through the dry areas of Australia, both in flocks of millions of birds.

In America passenger pigeons bred every year in great colonies. They were shot at the rate of up to a thousand a day for weeks during the years between 1870 and 1881. The birds were sold in the poultry markets in American cities. The last passenger pigeon in the wild was shot in Wisconsin in 1899, and the very last one died in a Cincinnati zoo in 1914. All that remains of these birds is a few museum specimens and a bronze tablet in Wyalsing State Park with a legend that reads:

★ DEDICATED TO THE LAST WISCONSIN ★
PASSENGER PIGEON
SHOT AT BABCOCK, SEPTEMBER 1899

THIS SPECIES BECAME EXTINCT
THROUGH THE AVARICE AND
THOUGHTLESSNESS OF MAN

ERECTED BY
THE WISCONSIN SOCIETY
★ FOR ORNITHOLOGY ★

In Australia the flock pigeons bred only after the rains fell and then nested so close to one another that one hunter killed 42 birds with a single shot. By 1910 Australians had turned most of the wild grass fields into sheep pastures and very few flock pigeons were seen. The flock pigeon was luckier than the passenger pigeon. Large sections of Australia are still wild, and a few years ago more than 2,000 still survived far from sheep and men.

Other well-known pigeons are the TURTLE DOVE of Europe, a favorite of poets, the WHITE-CROWNED PIGEON of the West Indies and the Florida Keys, the little BLEEDING HEART PIGEON of the Philippines, a favorite cage and zoo bird, and the JAMBU FRUIT DOVE of Malaysia whose colors rival the rainbow.

See also: DOMESTIC BIRDS

White-crowned Pigeon

Passenger Pigeon

♂

Pipits

Yellow Wagtail

Sprague's Pipit

These 54 species of 5- to 8-inch-long birds spend most of their lives walking and running along the ground looking for insects. They never hop. They live all over the world in arctic tundras, open fields, and mountain plateaus.

SPRAGUE'S PIPIT, the only completely American pipit, breeds from Minnesota west through Montana and across the border into Canada. It winters from Mississippi southward through Mexico. The 8 double notes of the male's spring song are high and clear. He sings continually while circling for an hour or more, sev-

eral hundred feet up in the air. Sprague's pipit builds a woven grass cup-nest which holds 4 or 5 purple-spotted gray eggs.

The WATER PIPIT breeds in the far north and on high mountains in the Northern Hemisphere around the world. It winters south into Central America, southern Asia, and North Africa.

Wagtails are Old World pipits that flick their tails up and down as they walk. The YELLOW WAGTAIL is common throughout Eurasia. It winters as far south as South Africa and southern India.

Plovers

The 63 plovers are shore birds. They are cousins of the sandpipers and oyster-catchers, but a number of them have left the sea and live inland. Their normal diet of insects, worms, snails, grubs, slugs, cutworms, beetles, maggots, caterpillars, insect eggs, and berries can be found in any bare open land that has not been sprayed with insecticides.

At the edge of the waves on sandy beaches, on mud flats, gravelly waste lands, or open pastures, plovers run swiftly on their 3 front toes. They have only a small bump or nothing where

their back toe should be. Holding their short tails straight behind and pointing their bills straight ahead, they fly strongly on long wings. As they fly, they call shrilly to each other and whistle tuneful notes. Many migrate vast distances over land and sea.

Plovers nest on the bare ground and lay from 2 to 5 eggs. The eggs are tan or gray, speckled with black, so like the color of the sand or soil under them that they are hard to see.

Plovers are devoted parents. When an intruder approaches eggs or chicks, the adult bird on guard tries to draw attention away from them. It flutters in another direction with one wing hanging as though broken. It may drag both wings or pretend it has a broken leg. A man or a fox following what he supposes is a wounded bird is lured far from the nest. This play-acting is a plover family trait. The parent plover is actually exposing itself and risking its own life for the safety of its young. Other birds that pretend injury in this way are oystercatchers, curlews, some species of pigeons, and some ducks.

The SURFBIRD and the KILLDEER are other plover names. Lapwings are Old World plovers that wear crests or wattles on their heads and often have spurs on their wings.

The most common and well-known plover in America is the killdeer. It breeds from central Canada to central Mexico, and the northernmost birds mi-grate in winter as far south as Peru. Away from the sea and often away from the water, the killdeer nests and lives in meadows, pastures, and plowed land where grass is scant and low. Bare places at the edges of railroad tracks and roads are favorite spots. Each pair nests alone but they travel in flocks in winter. Favorites of the farmer because they devour beetles, grasshoppers, and cutworms, they announce their presence by half-sad, half-scolding "kill-dee, kill-dee, kill-dee" calls all year round.

In Eurasia the EUROPEAN LAPWING is an upland plover like the killdeer. Its call is an often repeated "pee-witt." Its eggs are collected and sold in Europe. It lays a second set if the first is taken away early in the nesting season. In southern Africa, the CROWNED LAPWING, the noisiest bird in Africa, takes the European lapwing's place in the fields.

GOLDEN PLOVERS are long-distance

Killdeer

Ruddy Turnstone

78

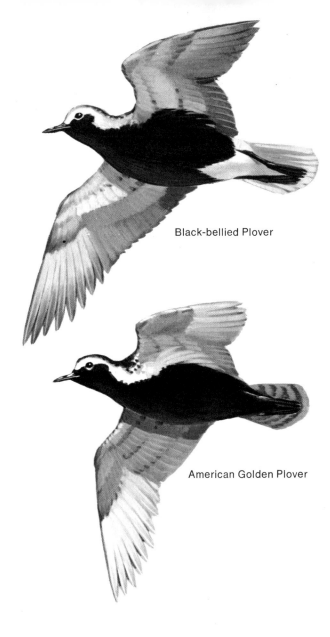

Black-bellied Plover

American Golden Plover

fliers. They breed on Arctic Ocean islands around the pole and winter as far south as Australia. Each fall one group flies 2,000 miles nonstop from Alaska to the Hawaiian Islands, and returns in spring. Those that winter in New Zealand and Australia breed on Siberian islands. Golden plovers stay along the shore and feed at low tide. The RUDDY TURNSTONE has the same range as the golden plover and like that bird migrates in great flocks. In Australia it feeds with the golden plover along the shore but in Hawaii it feeds on the uplands.

The BLACK-BELLIED PLOVER, known as the GRAY PLOVER in the Old World, travels in small groups from the Arctic to its wintering grounds. It does not go to Hawaii, but some black-bellied plovers winter along the southern coasts of southern North America as do some ruddy turnstones. The 12-inch-long black-belly is the largest American plover.

The WRYBILL PLOVER of New Zealand has developed a crooked bill. It is the only bird in the world that can reach around rocks for hidden insects. Young wrybill plovers are able to swim when only 1 or 2 days old.

Prairie Chickens
See Grouse

Ptarmigans
See Feathers; Gallinaceous Birds; Grouse

Puffins
See Auks

Quails
See Pheasants

Quetzal
See Trogons

Lapwing

Rails

The 132 species of rails include coots, gallinules, crakes, moorhens, and wood-rails. They live in temperate and tropical zones all over the world. The WATER RAIL of the warmer parts of Eurasia also breeds near hot springs in Iceland, unusually far north for a rail. Another, the VIRGINIA RAIL, breeds from southern Canada south to the Straits of Magellan, unusually far south for a rail.

Rails all have slim, narrow bodies so they can slip between reeds and grasses on their long legs and long toes without rustling a leaf or a blade. "Thin as a rail," they can move about yet remain hidden. In the salt-water marshes of the United States the SORA RAIL, the CLAPPER RAIL, and the VIRGINIA RAIL are game birds. Hunters wait until high tides flood the marshes so the rails cannot slip away from them but must fly to escape. The rail takes off into the air weakly, straight up between the reeds and grasses. This makes him an easy target. The KING RAIL lives in fresh-water marshes and is harder to hunt because there are no tides to drive it out of hiding.

Most of the rail family breed on or near the water. They make simple grass or reed nests on clumps of marsh grass or floating plants, a few inches to a foot above water. Sometimes they build right on the wet swampy ground. The AMERICAN COOT and the OLD WORLD COOT often hide their floating nests in thick rushes or reeds. Coots have scalloped toes that help them swim. So do gallinules.

The COMMON GALLINULE, known as the COMMON MOORHEN in Europe, builds an entrance runway of reeds to its floating nest. The people of Hawaii say the common gallinule has a horny red shield above its bill because it was burned when it brought the gift of fire to the islands. They call it the ALAE, meaning burned forehead. The common gallinule lives all over the warm world but not in Australia or New Zealand.

Some rails have developed odd ways of nesting. The BONAPARTES' HORNED

Sora Rail

Clapper Rail

American Coot

COOT of the Andes mountain lakes, where few plants grow, builds a mound of stones on which to lay its eggs. The mated pair carry pebbles, a little larger than walnuts, in their bills to shallow water or a protected spot on shore.

The CORN CRAKE that breeds in Eurasia and winters through Africa is not a marsh bird; it lives in the uplands and makes a grass cup-nest in hay or grainfields. It migrates thousands of miles and, like all rails, travels at night. Like all night-flying migrants, it probably navigates by the stars.

The CAYENNE WOODRAIL of Central and South America is a bird of the marshy woodlands as are all woodrails. It builds a deep bowl-nest of small twigs often lined with bamboo leaves 3 to 20 feet above ground. It is found in woods near fresh-water streams and also in mangrove trees over salt water.

Most of the rail family take only 1 mate and raise 2 broods of from 6 to 16 young each year. The downy, dark chicks hatch from white, tan, or olive-colored brown-speckled eggs. The chicks leave the nest right after hatching. They are guarded and cared for by the parents.

Often the young of the earlier brood help care for the second brood.

A number of rails, most of them living on islands, have lost the ability to fly. Many of these have become extinct during this century. The little 6-inch-long LAYSAN ISLAND RAIL was wiped out by rats that came ashore from navy ships during World War II. The NOTORNIS, a big 24-inch-long flightless gallinule of New Zealand, was known only from a few birds collected long ago. The last one was shot in 1898, after which the bird was thought to be extinct. But in 1948 it was rediscovered in some wild valleys of the unexplored Murchison Mountains. The female notornis never lays more than 4 eggs, sometimes only 2, each spring. With protection from the New Zealand government the notornis population may grow.

Most rails are solitary birds living alone, but coots and gallinules gather in flocks, especially on their wintering grounds. They feed and rest like ducks on the water in large groups. Rails feed on every eatable creature and plant they come upon. The American coot is the most plentiful and best known rail in America.

Corn Crake

Common Gallinule

Robins

The BRITISH ROBIN is a 5½-inch thrush and is known in much of Eurasia. The AMERICAN ROBIN is an 8½-inch thrush that is known from Alaska to Guatemala.

A mated pair of American robins usually take about a week to build their mud-plastered, grass-lined, twig nest. The male helps to bring material but the female does the building. A pair have been known to finish a nest in a day. But bad weather can keep them from finishing for more than 2 weeks. The female incubates the 3 or 4 blue eggs for 11 to 14 days. The chicks are naked when hatched. In about 2 weeks they grow feathers and leave the nest. The male parent feeds the chicks and shows them how to pull worms out of the ground for some days after the nest is empty.

See also: THRUSHES

Sandpipers

See Snipes

Sapsuckers

See Woodpeckers

Shearwaters

See Petrels

British Robin

American Robin

These are 7- to 10-inch perching birds that hunt like hawks but kill with their beaks instead of their claws. They prey on insects, small birds, frogs, lizards, mice, and other small rodents. They often hang their catch on a thorn when prey is plentiful and return to eat it when prey is scarce. Because they hang their meat as a butcher does, they are sometimes called "butcher-birds."

The NORTHERN SHRIKE breeds in Alaska and northern Canada in the New World, and in northern Europe and Siberia in the Old. If mice and birds are scarce in winter, it may wander as far south as Texas hunting for food. It builds a bulky nest each spring, often in evergreen trees. The female lays 4 to 6 gray eggs. The male's songs are much like those of the mockingbird.

The LOGGERHEAD SHRIKE breeds from southern Canada through Mexico. It migrates in winter only from the northern part of its range. It eats insects more than anything else, particularly in the southern states and Mexico. It often hunts from a perch or the telephone wires along the highways. It sometimes hangs its kill on the barbs of barbed wire fences. The male loggerhead has a song in spring but his calls are harsh. These birds like to nest high in thorny trees. They raise 4 to 6 chicks each year. Their eggs are white with gray speckling.

The 62 other kinds of shrikes are found in Eurasia and Africa. Some of the African shrikes, unlike our gray bird, wear bright colors like the MANY-COLORED BUSH-SHRIKE. It is as gay as a Christmas tree ornament but so shy that its nest and eggs have never been discovered.

Northern Shrike

Loggerhead Shrike

Many-colored Bush-shrike

♂

Black Skimmer

Skimmers

A skimmer's bill looks like a pair of embroidery scissors, $3\frac{1}{2}$ to 4 inches long, with a shortened top blade. Skimmers fly just above the water with the bigger bottom blade of their bills cutting through the surface, and the short top blade ready to clamp down on a fish. Strong neck muscles make it possible for skimmers to jerk the fish free of the water and swallow it without missing a wing-beat. A skimmer's long wings beat slowly, and always well above the bird's body so they never touch the water. Skimmers start fishing at dusk and stop when the sun rises even though the pupils of their eyes are oblong and can be narrowed to slits to protect them from light. During the day skimmers sit in flocks dozing on the beaches.

Skimmers breed in colonies on the open beach. The 2 to 5 eggs are laid on the sand. The female incubates them alone. The chicks hatch covered with grayish, sand-colored down and with both blades of their scissorlike bills the same length. Their coloring is a protection. They are hard to see on the beach.

When a male skimmer courts a female he often walks in front of her with a stick in his bill. If the female grabs the stick, she accepts him as her mate. If she pays no attention to the stick the male knows he has been refused.

The BLACK SKIMMER is found on the Atlantic Coast from New York to the southern tip of South America and on South America's Pacific Coast. This 18-inch bird is the largest of the 3 skimmers. An inch or two smaller, the INDIAN SKIMMER lives on rivers from India to Burma and Indochina. The AFRICAN SKIMMER is only 14 inches long. It lives on lakes, rivers, and ponds south of the Sahara Desert.

This family takes its name from the only bird in the world that nests within both the Arctic and the Antarctic Circles, the SKUA. The other 3 species in the group are all Arctic Coast breeders. They are the PARASITIC JAEGER, the POMARINE JAEGER, and the LONG-TAILED JAEGER. *Jaeger* is a German word meaning hunter, and all the birds in this family are hunters. They swoop down on small mammals, large insects, fish, shellfish, young and old birds, birds' eggs, and, when they find them, the carcasses of dead animals.

In Antarctica the skua nests near Adelie penguin colonies and feeds its 1 or 2 chicks on penguin eggs and penguin chicks. In the Arctic it nests near gull or petrel colonies and preys on their eggs and young. In Antarctica a pair of skuas often destroy their second chick and only raise the first hatchling. In the Arctic they usually raise both chicks.

Parasitic jaegers place their nests close together in large colonies. Long-tailed jaegers nest some distance from one another in small colonies. Pomarine jaegers scatter far apart to nest over the swampy tundra. All jaeger nests are rounded hollows in the ground or moss. The females usually lay their 2 eggs in June. Cared for by both parents, the young leave the nest in 2 days. They fly before they are a month old, but the parents feed them for another 10 days or so after they fly. A great part of their food is the little arctic mammal called lemming. Jaegers often obtain food by attacking flying terns and gulls and forcing them to give up a catch of fish. The jaegers snatch it from the air as it falls.

The skua family all leave the icy waters of the polar regions during the cold months. The three jaegers and the arctic-breeding skua winter at sea in temperate and subtropical oceans. The antarctic-breeding skua winters at sea in the southern oceans. Until they are 3 years old and ready to mate, the young birds stay on the wintering ground the year around. Their shrill, harsh, or rasping cries are heard when they feed together and on their nesting grounds.

Long-tailed Jaeger

Skua

Snipes

This gathering of 82 species of shore birds includes sandpipers, curlews, whimbrels, godwits, willets, snipes, woodcocks, stints, knots, yellowlegs, dowitchers, tattlers, redshanks, surfbirds, and others. All of them walk and wade on longish to very long legs. They fly without effort on long pointed wings. Their slender bills are longer than their heads, some as much as four times as long. Many bills are straight, but some are down-curved. Some of the snipe-sandpiper family, like the 24-inch-long LONG-BILLED CURLEW of North America, are as big as a good-sized chicken but much more graceful. Some, like the 6-inch-long LEAST SAND-PIPER of America, are the size of a house sparrow.

Most of the snipe family breed in the Northern Hemisphere. Those that breed on islands and coasts in the Arctic Circle migrate great distances to winter in the Southern Hemisphere. Common species that do this in the New World are the GREATER and LESSER YELLOW-LEGS, the WHITE-RUMPED SANDPIPER, the DOWITCHER, the MARBLED GODWIT, and the SEMI-PALMATED SANDPIPER. Common

species that do this in the Old World are the RUFF and his mate the REEVE, the LITTLE STINT, and the REDSHANK. Common species that do this in both the New World and the Old World are the COMMON SNIPE, the WHIMBREL, the KNOT, the DUNLIN, and the SANDERLING.

Others of the snipe-sandpiper family do not fly so far. The AMERICAN WOODCOCK breeds and migrates in eastern North America between southern Canada and the Gulf of Mexico. The SURFBIRD breeds in Alaska and winters along the Pacific Coast in North, Central, and South America. The SPOON-BILL SANDPIPER breeds in northeast Siberia and winters in southeast Asia. It probably has a special use for its odd-shaped bill, but no one has yet found out about it.

None of this group of wading birds builds a nest. They usually lay 4 dark-spotted, greenish or tan eggs in a hollow the bird makes by turning itself around as it sits on the bare ground. The eggs are incubated for 20 to 24 days depending on the species. The chicks hatch covered with soft down and able to run around, but usually stay in the nest-hole

Marbled Godwit

Willet

Whimbrel

for a day or so. A parent stays with them brooding them under its wings. The adult birds have fine flight calls and whistles when courting. They cluck to their young. The chicks cheep or "seep" for attention.

The breeding places of all the snipe-sandpiper family are marshes, mud flats, open fields, arctic tundras, and pastures, but nearly always near water. A few have left the water. One is the misnamed UP-LAND PLOVER. This is really a sandpiper that breeds on the prairies, in pastures, hayfields, and airports. It chooses places where food—grasshoppers, crickets, weevils—for its chicks is plentiful.

Every state and province of the United States and Canada has its visiting sandpipers in spring and fall. The birds migrate slowly, stopping to feed for days at a time on marshes, mud flats, open beaches and lake and river shores. Even mountain streams are visited by the WAN-DERING TATTLER that lays its eggs near them in Alaska. The surfbird breeds on mountain tops above the timberline in the same area. The SPOTTED SANDPIPER, which cannot seem to keep its tail from bobbing up and down, balances itself on rocks while hunting water creatures. It walks underwater on the bottom of streams like a dipper in mountains of North America.

In the 1800's and early 1900's, many hundreds of thousands of greater and lesser yellowlegs, knots, ESKIMO CURLEWS, WILLETS, and dowitchers were shot for the market. By 1922, their numbers had become so few that all but the common snipe and the American woodcock were put on the protected list. Sportsmen enjoy hunting snipe and woodcock because their darting flight makes them hard but interesting targets. These birds are about the size of a robin. When they are broiled, they shrink to just 1 or 2 mouthfuls but are delicious.

Modern sportsmen know that if they wish to hunt in the years to come they must limit their present shooting. Never again will a man boast as one did in the last century that he had killed 340 snipes in one day and rarely got less than 150 a day during the fall, winter, and spring. And he also was a so-called gentleman sportsman.

See also: PLOVERS

Long-billed Dowitcher

American Woodcock

Common Snipe

Sanderling

Song

See Voice

Sparrows and Related Birds

This is a group of more than 300 kinds of small perching, singing land birds. In addition to a number of species of mostly brownish sparrows, the family includes the more brightly feathered finches, juncos, grosbeaks, towhees, longspurs, saltators, and related buntings and siskins. Over 250 species live in North and South America. The remaining species are scattered over Europe, Asia, and Africa. In 1862 English settlers brought several kinds of finches and buntings into New Zealand and released them in the wild. Their descendants are plentiful there today.

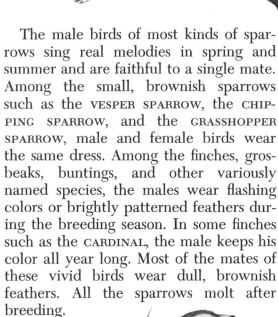

Ortolan Bunting

Vesper Sparrow

All sparrows have very short bills adapted for seed eating, but they also eat other plant material and some insects. Most sparrows fly strongly and travel long distances between their breeding and their wintering grounds. A few, like the nonmigrating SEASIDE SPARROWS of southern salt-water marshes of the United States, have a weak, fluttery flight.

The male birds of most kinds of sparrows sing real melodies in spring and summer and are faithful to a single mate. Among the small, brownish sparrows such as the VESPER SPARROW, the CHIPPING SPARROW, and the GRASSHOPPER SPARROW, male and female birds wear the same dress. Among the finches, grosbeaks, buntings, and other variously named species, the males wear flashing colors or brightly patterned feathers during the breeding season. In some finches such as the CARDINAL, the male keeps his color all year long. Most of the mates of these vivid birds wear dull, brownish feathers. All the sparrows molt after breeding.

Savannah Sparrow

The 4¾-inch-long SAVANNAH SPARROW ranges over a larger territory than any other member of its family. It breeds from northern Alaska to Arizona and West Virginia. It winters southward, throughout Central America.

Buntings, towhees, juncos, dickcissels,

Chipping Sparrow

Grasshopper Sparrow

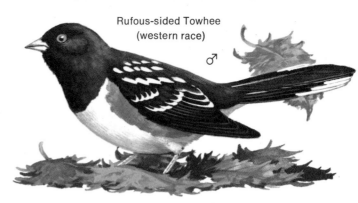
Rufous-sided Towhee
(western race)
♂

and most of the brownish sparrows build a cup-shaped nest of stems and grasses. It is well hidden on or close to the ground. The females lay 3 to 5 greenish-blue eggs, speckled with darker colors. Often the females build the nests and incubate the eggs alone. But the male birds help feed the chicks with insects and seeds, and protect the nest and young from intruders.

Song Sparrow

The SONG SPARROW is well named because no other American sparrow sings oftener or longer or knows as many melodies. It builds its first nest each spring when the trees are bare and places it on the ground. After the leaves come out it builds in shrubs or trees 4 or 5 feet or more above the ground. A song sparrow may live to be 8 years old and breeds, as do all sparrows, when it is one year old.

Gray-crowned
Rosy Finch
♂

The grosbeaks and finches nest 4 to 60 feet above the ground, except the GRAY-CROWNED ROSY FINCH. It breeds in the far north and in high mountains where trees are scarce. It places its nest in rock crevices. The HOUSE FINCH of the western states uses any sort of a bird box or any sort of protected hole it can find, even an old oriole's nest. The other finches build well-woven nests in trees or shrubs.

The RUFOUS-SIDED TOWHEE of southernmost Canada and the United States calls its name "to-whee" from shrubs and brush. In searching for seeds and insects, it hops and kicks with both feet at once. In nests built by the female close to or on the ground, a pair of rufous-sided towhees raise 2 broods of young each summer. Many times they also raise a brown-headed cowbird chick. The GREEN-TAILED TOWHEE nests 9,000 feet above sea level in the Rocky Mountains and winters in northern Mexico.

Two widespread Eurasian species are the CHAFFINCH, a bird of hedges, gardens, and parks, and the BRAMBLING. The brambling is a finch that nests in the birch forests of the north, and winters in the British Isles and south to the Mediterranean Sea and Japan.

The largest sparrows are the 10½-inch saltators of Central and South America. These birds eat fruit, berries, and flowers more often than seeds. They raise several broods of 2 chicks each during the year.

According to the European cookbooks the most delicious eating of the sparrows is the ORTOLAN BUNTING. Since ancient times, it has been netted during fall migration when it is very fat. It is eaten in every country in Europe except Britain where it does not occur. That is why Europe has few buntings left.

See also: BUNTINGS; CARDINALS; FINCHES; GROSBEAKS

Brambling

Spoonbills

The bills of these wading birds are the shape of the flat wooden spoons that come with paper cups of ice cream. When feeding, a spoonbill walks with its tail in the air and its head and feet in the mud. It moves its half-open bill sideways back and forth until it has caught a little fish, a water insect, a small shrimp, or a fiddler crab. Then it raises its head, closes its bill, and moves the top and bottom of the bill against one another as though chewing its catch. With a final shake of the bill it swallows the catch. Spoonbills feed at night in shallow salt-water bays and inlets at low tide. They rest during the day standing in large flocks at the edge of the water.

Spoonbills are a branch of the ibis family. They evolved from the same ancestor and have the same general habits. No one knows why they developed the odd-shaped bills and night-hunting that makes them seem different from the ibises.

There are 6 species of spoonbills in the world, 1 in southern Eurasia, 1 in Asia, 1 in Africa, 2 in Australia, and 1 in the Americas. The glamorous, glowing ROSE-ATE SPOONBILL was once as common as the sea gulls on the coasts of southern Florida, Louisiana and southern Texas. A hundred years ago men shot roseate spoonbills by the thousand to make fans of their beautiful wings. Now only a few small flocks live in National Parks and Refuges. Larger numbers survive in Central and South America.

The other 5 species of spoonbills are all more or less white birds.

The YELLOW-BILLED SPOONBILL of Australia has a bright yellow unfeathered face that matches its yellow bill and legs, and beautiful plumelike feathers on its back.

See also: IBISES

Roseate Spoonbill

Starlings

Indian Hill Myna

Common Starling

Yellow-billed Oxpecker

Superb Starling

This family of 106 Old World perching birds wears silky dark feathers that shine like metal in sunlight or glisten like the stars they were named for. Some from tropical Asia and Africa carry bright crests or wattles on their heads. From 7 to 17 inches long, they are chunky birds that walk and run with a waddle on strong legs and feet. They fly straight and fast and most migrate.

Starlings fly, roost, breed, and feed in groups. They chitter-chatter to each other, whistle, and warble all day long and sometimes at night. Many species are natural mimics.

Starlings breed in many different ways. Some species, like the SUPERB STARLING of Africa, build dome-shaped nests, covered with thorny twigs, lined with feathers, hair, or fine grass, with a side entrance. Some species nest in holes in trees, some in holes in earth banks, some—in Africa—in holes in termite nests, some in rock crevices, and some on cliff ledges. The GLOSSY STARLING of the South Pacific builds a nest similar to those of social weaverbirds. On a lone tree in a clearing 50 or more of these nests hang so close to each other they seem woven together. The twitter of the birds occupying them is loud enough to be heard half a mile away. Some species, like the RED-WING STARLING of Africa, build a bulky loose nest in the crown of a palm tree. Some use the discarded nests of other birds.

Starling eggs may be blue or white, plain or spotted. Usually 4 or 5 are laid at each nesting but some species lay as few as 2 and some have been known to lay as many as 9 eggs. Some starlings raise 3 broods of chicks a year. The eggs are incubated by the females, sometimes with male help. The males always help feed the chicks. Starlings feed their young on insects and more than 50 percent of adult starling food is insects. Starlings also eat fruit, grain, table scraps, other birds' eggs, shellfish, and lizards. They like stale bread.

Two species of starlings are well known in America. One is the COMMON STARLING; the other is the INDIAN HILL MYNA.

The common starling is native to Eurasia and northern Africa but is found everywhere except South America and Hawaii. It did not fly around the world, but was carried by man to all places where grain and fruit grow and Englishmen settled. Instead of eating nuisance insects it has become a nuisance itself in North America, Australia, New Zealand, South Africa, and many ocean islands.

In North America the 120 common starlings released in Central Park in New

91

York City in 1890–91 had 120,000,000 descendants in 1965. In great flocks they range from the Atlantic to the Pacific and from southern Canada into northern Mexico. These noisy, quarrelsome birds move into cities in winter to roost at night on buildings and trees. They mar the buildings and damage the trees with their droppings. Their loud chattering increases when they nest on building ledges and crevices to raise their 4 or 5 squeaking chicks. In the country they take every sort of nesting place of all our native birds, including bluebird birdhouses. If they can find no other spot, they use the ground and build large untidy homes on it. Their appetite for soft fruit, corn, wheat, oats, and young sprouting garden vegetables makes the farmer their enemy. The fact that they eat harmful Japanese beetles, grasshoppers, and caterpillars does not make up for swallowing other birds' eggs and eating all the cherries on a tree.

The shade-loving Indian hill myna is native to the forests of India, Ceylon, Burma, and parts of Malaysia. In large flocks it flies in the tops of teakwood trees and is commonly seen in shade trees on coffee plantations. It eats fruit and insects and sips nectar from blooms of the bombox and other flowering trees. It lays its 2 or 3 eggs in a hole high up in a dead tree too rotten for man to climb. If no natural hole can be found, the Indian hill myna digs its own with its stout bill. In years past thousands of these whistling mimics were shipped from Calcutta and Rangoon to pet shops all over the world. Most Indian hill mynas now sold in America are raised here in captivity. They are one of the best talking birds. The COMMON MYNA of southern Asia does not learn to talk well but pet shops often sell both species without knowing the difference. The hill myna can be recognized by its glossy-black plumage with tints of green and purple in the sun. The common myna is dark brown.

Two African starlings are called the RED-BILLED OXPECKER and the YELLOW-BILLED OXPECKER from their habit of riding on the backs of oxen, rhinoceroses, giraffes, and other large animals. The birds eat the ticks that fasten themselves onto all African mammals. Hunters dislike the oxpeckers because the birds always warn the animal they are riding of approaching danger. The oxpeckers raise their bills and hiss a loud alarm call and away goes the antelope the hunter was about to shoot.

Storks

In northern Europe the WHITE STORKS return from Africa every spring. Faithfully, for 20 years or more each pair goes to its own old nest on the roof of some building, castle, cottage, or skyscraper. Male and female working together repair the nest, adding new sticks, branches, mud, grass, moss, rags, paper, and feathers. Sharing all the duties of parent birds, they raise 3 to 5 young storks, feeding them for several weeks after they learn to fly. The chicks hatch with small black bills that grow as the birds grow and turn red when the birds are full-grown. The young storks are fond of the nest and roost on it nights until they leave for Africa in the fall.

Danes, Germans, and the Dutch believe the white stork is an example of happy family life, that it guards the house on which it nests, and brings good luck to the people within. In many fables and legends, the stork is said to drop new babies down the chimney. From these

Wood Stork

Adjutant Stork

Saddlebill Stork

tales we have the common expression "a visit from the stork," meaning a child has been born.

Across Eurasia where the white stork lives near man, the BLACK STORK lives far from him on rocky cliffs and tall trees. There are no legends about black storks.

Only one of the 17 different kinds of storks is found in North America. The WOOD STORK, often mistakenly called the wood ibis, breeds plentifully in the swamps from South Carolina to Florida and Texas. Like all storks it has long legs for wading in shallow waters and a long strong bill for catching fish, reptiles, and amphibians. It is particularly fond of frogs and will take any sort of insect. The wood stork nests in colonies in the upper branches of giant swamp trees, such as bald cypress.

If too many swamps are drained Americans will only see this bird again by traveling to Central and South American swamps.

Storks are all big birds from 30 inches to the 60-inch-long ADJUTANT or MARABOU STORK of tropical Africa. The adjutant carries around a long pouch covered with bare pink skin. It hangs from the bird's throat and probably has something to do with its breathing. The adjutant competes with vultures for carrion, eating any dead creature it finds. It is nearly as tall as the SADDLEBILL, also found in Africa.

A number of storks have patches of bare skin. The wood stork's black head is completely bare of feathers. The JABIRU STORK, found from Mexico south to Argentina, has an equally bare black head. One of the gayest storks is the PAINTED STORK of southern Asia. Its bare orange face and enormous yellow bill can be seen for long distances on the mud flats and rice paddies where it hunts and fishes. It nests and perches on trees. On the inland marshes of southern Asia the OPEN-BILLED STORK uses its pincer-shaped bill to crush fresh-water shellfish.

93

Swallows

These 4- to 9-inch-long dark graceful birds spend most of their waking hours on the wing. All day long all 79 species swoop through the air with mouths wide open, catching flying insects in much the same way the nightjars do after dark. Like nightjars they grow bristles around their mouths that help them gather in the insects. Swallow wings are long and pointed and carry the birds high into the air and on long migrations.

The BARN SWALLOW, the CLIFF SWALLOW, the CAVE SWALLOW, the VIOLET-GREEN SWALLOW, the TREE SWALLOW, the BANK SWALLOW, the ROUGH-WINGED SWALLOW, and the PURPLE MARTIN all breed in North America, some as far north as Alaska and the shores of Hudson Bay. They all winter southward. The tree swallow migrates into Central America, the others into South America to Brazil and Argentina. The BAHAMA SWALLOW sometimes wanders into Florida from its Caribbean home and the GRAY-BREASTED MARTIN sometimes wanders into Texas from its Central and South American home. Scientists call these birds "accidentals." When they appear in North America they have usually been carried out of their way by the high winds of hurricanes.

The barn swallow and the bank swallow breed in Eurasia as well as in North America. In England they are called the COMMON SWALLOW and the SAND MARTIN. From Europe and northern Asia these birds fly to Africa and southern Asia for the winter. The HOUSE MARTIN is another Old World swallow that travels the same path.

In addition to the Eurasian swallows that winter in Africa, a number are native there. The STRIPED SWALLOW is unusual among swallows because it has a streaked breast. So does the LARGER STRIPED SWALLOW, also of Africa.

Australia is the home of a number of swallows, the TREE MARTIN, the FAIRY MARTIN, and the WELCOME SWALLOW. New Zealand has no native swallow.

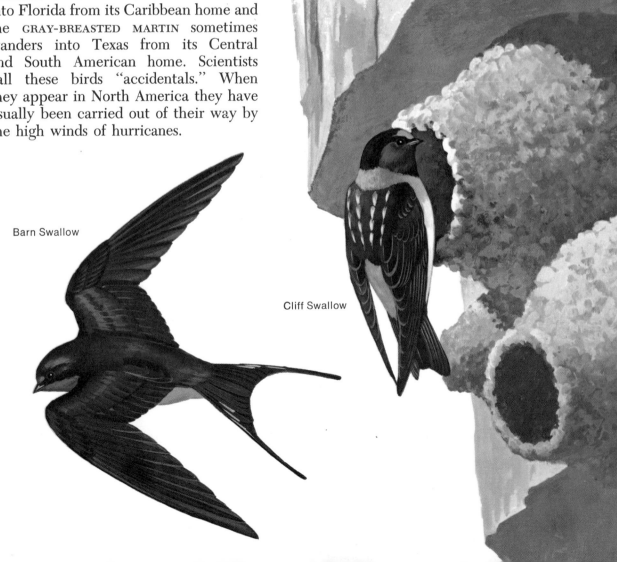

Barn Swallow

Cliff Swallow

Swallows have weak little feet with curly front toes grown together at the base so they can perch but find it difficult to walk. In late summer and fall along America's highways one can often see gatherings of hundreds of tree swallows, bank swallows or barn swallows perched on telephone wires.

Swallows all twitter. A few, like the cliff and bank swallows, give squeaky, buzzing twitters. Some, like the purple martin, twitter musically. Swallows twitter at their nests and, since many of them nest in colonies, they can make a lot of noise. Some species breed in natural hollows in trees or under rocks. Some dig burrows in sand banks or cliffs and many build mud nests, either cup-shaped or bottle-shaped.

The $4\frac{3}{4}$-inch fairy martins build a mud nest which may weigh from $1\frac{1}{2}$ to $2\frac{3}{4}$ pounds. An Australian observer says that one male bird carried 1,300 pellets of mud to the female who did the building. The bottle was about 6 inches in diameter and the neck-shaped entrance 6 inches long. It was one of a colony of 30 nests hanging on a cliff. On a pillow of feathers and grass inside the bottle the birds lay 3 sets of 4 or 5 white eggs in Australia's spring.

Many swallows have left cliffs and hollow trees for man-made nesting sites. The American purple martins once nested under rocks. They left the rocks for gourds that the Indians hung for them in their villages. They live now in highrise apartment houses with rooms for 20 pairs or more in suburban gardens. Barn swallows use the rafters of barns, garages, and other buildings to hold their mud and grass cups. They have left the hollow trees and so have the tree swallows. A colony of tree swallows will come to bird houses on poles or tall fence posts scattered 12 to every 3 acres. They will pay their rent by feeding their chicks on mosquitoes. The Eurasian house martin hangs its nest under the eaves of buildings.

Eskimo children love the cliff swallows that build bottle-shaped mud nests on the sea cliffs in Alaska. They believe they are the spirits of children who once built playhouse igloos in the same places.

Tree Swallow

Purple Martin
♂

Swans

See Waterfowl

Swifts

A bird that can fly 100 miles an hour is well named "swift." One of the larger swifts, the 8-inch BROWN-THROATED NEEDLE-TAILED SWIFT of Asia, has reached that speed. Many of the 67 kinds of swifts can fly up to 70 miles an hour, but a large group of little cave swiftlets of Asia fly slowly. Cave swiftlets flutter about like butterflies, changing direction every few seconds.

Swifts spend more time in the air than any other land birds. Sometimes they even remain on the wing all night. Swifts cannot walk, hop, or run, nor can they perch on a limb. When they rest at night they hang from their very small but strong hook-shaped toes on the walls of cliffs, caves, canyons, hollow trees, and chimneys. Most of them prop their short tails against the wall and let their long wings trail on either side of themselves.

Fourteen swifts of Asia and Africa and the New World CHIMNEY SWIFT and VAUX'S SWIFT are known as needle-tailed swifts. The tips of their tail feathers end in needlelike points. When these birds cling to the inside walls of hollow trees their needle-ended tail feathers stick into the wood like pins in a pin cushion. The needle tails help to steady the birds as they hang.

Swifts' bills are tiny but their mouths are large. They fly with mouths gaping open and catch insects in the same way that swallows and nightjars do. They grow no bristles around their mouths. When a swift hunts insects to feed its chicks it fills its mouth and cheeks with them.

Swifts glue their nests of plant material and feathers together with a sticky spit made in a gland in their throats. Some swifts make their nest entirely of this spit. The needle-tailed swifts lay from 3 to 5 white eggs each year in nests the shape of a half a cup, glued to the inside wall of a hollow tree or chimney. Other

Chimney Swift

swifts lay 1 or 2 white eggs each year on a narrow shelf or flat pad, and glue their eggs to it. The needle-tailed swifts, the COMMON SWIFT of Europe and a few other swifts incubate by sitting on their nests. Many swifts hang from the wall over their eggs to incubate them. The swift chicks can cling to the nest or wall as soon as they hatch. They do not leave the nest site until they can fly well, after from 4 to 6 weeks. If a young swift falls from the wall before its wings are strong, it cannot rise again.

In America the chimney swift breeds in the eastern United States from southern Canada through Florida and eastern Texas. Vaux's swift and the BLACK SWIFT breed on the West Coast. Vaux's swift breeds in hollow trees, redwoods and others, in forests from Alaska to central California. The black swift breeds in canyons and on walls behind waterfalls in the mountains and on sea cliffs from Alaska to southern California. The WHITE-THROATED SWIFT has more white feathers than any other American swift. It breeds in the high mountains of western America. It nests in cracks in cliffs from southern Canada to southwestern New Mexico. The white-throated swift is the fastest flyer of the North American swifts.

All the swifts that breed in the Northern Hemisphere winter in the tropics. Swifts cannot live without insects, which are killed by cold. So swifts leave their northern breeding grounds long before the first frost, soon after their young are on the wing. Northern Old World swifts go to tropical Asia and Africa. Northern New World swifts go to tropical Central and South America. Swifts that breed in the tropics do not migrate.

Most interesting and valuable swifts are 3 of the cave swiftlets of southeast Asia—LOW'S SWIFTLET, the GRAY-RUMPED SWIFTLET, and the BROWN-RUMPED SWIFTLET. These birds build the nests from which the Chinese make their famous bird's-nest soup.

Swiftlets find their way in the dark caves they live in by listening to the echo of their own chirping calls.

Low's Swiftlet

Black Swift

Tanagers

All 222 species of tanagers are native to the warmer parts of the Americas. All but 4 breed in the tropics and stay near their breeding places the year around. The 4 that breed in North America are the SCARLET, the SUMMER, the HEPATIC, and the WESTERN TANAGERS. After breeding these birds all migrate to winter in the tropics. Tanagers wear bright clear colors: reds, yellows, blues, and greens with patches of black or white. Most males and females dress alike, but not the 4 North American species whose females wear drab yellowish olive-green and black.

Some tanagers are as large as American robins. Some are small as a house wren. Some have plumage that looks like velvet. Some have plumage of changeable colors. In spite of their weak songs, tanagers were once favorite cage birds. The BLUE-GRAY TANAGER from tropical America escaped from cages in southern Florida and now nests in the Miami area. The many-colored SUPERB TANAGER, the CHESTNUT-HEADED CALLISTA, and the little VIOLET EUPHONIA and his drab mate from South America are all popular tanagers in European pet shops. The velvety male SCARLET-RUMPED TANAGER, with its silver bill and glowing red eyes, is brought to Europe, but his drab mate is left behind in the Central America scrublands. This tanager sings, but not a true melody.

Tanagers eat fruit, flowers, and insects. They build shallow, loosely woven cup-nests in trees or bushes and some add roofs and side entrances. The females lay clutches of 1 to 5 eggs. The North American tanagers' eggs are a dark speckled bluish green. Some tropical species lay white eggs. The eggs are incubated by the females for about two weeks. The chicks are fed and brooded by both parents. In the tropics many tanagers raise 2 and 3 broods of chicks each nesting season.

Scarlet Tanager ♂

Western Tanager ♂

Scarlet Tanager
♀

Terns

See Gulls

Thrashers

See Mockingbirds

Thrushes

Nightingale

Thrushes live in almost every country in the world where insects creep and crawl and wild fruits grow. These well-loved birds sing truly beautiful songs full of bubbling notes in gardens, parks, orchards, pastures, woodlands, fields, and along country roadsides. Some thrushes, such as the Old World NIGHTINGALE, sing day and night. Some thrushes, such as the American TOWNSEND'S SOLITAIRE, sing all year long, warbling and trilling their ringing notes from treetop perches and from the air. Some thrushes, such as GRAY'S ROBIN of Central America, sing so sweetly and so often that Costa Ricans capture it to keep in cages.

The Old World SONG THRUSH's loud musical voice is so loved by Europeans that they have carried this bird to New Zealand where thrushes were not native. It is now more plentiful there than many of New Zealand's own birds. The song thrush has also been carried to Australia, where it is as much at home as the SCRUB-ROBIN, Australia's own thrush. The song thrush may some day be more

99

plentiful than the scrub-robin because the imported bird raises 2 or 3 broods of 4 or 5 young a year and the scrub-robin raises only 1 chick a year. Several thrushes have been introduced into Hawaii where the native thrushes became extinct around 1900. When introduced into countries where they are not native, thrushes have never become nuisances as have starlings and house sparrows.

Of the 11 thrushes that breed in North America, 5 look much alike. They are brown birds, 6 to 7 inches long, with spotted breasts—the VEERY, the HERMIT THRUSH, SWAINSON'S THRUSH, the WOOD THRUSH, and the GRAY-CHEEKED THRUSH. The wood thrush stays in the east from southern Canada to the Gulf of Mexico. The others are more widespread. So is the American robin. The VARIED THRUSH of the West Coast that resembles the robin, Townsend's solitaire of the western woods, and the three bluebirds each have their own range. These 11 thrushes winter in Central America and some go to South America. The American robin breeds from the tree line in Alaska and Canada to the Gulf of Mexico. In winter it is seen from the Canadian border through Florida and Mexico to Guatemala.

Swainson's Thrushes

Hermit Thrush

Central and South America have a large number of thrushes of their own. The GREAT THRUSH of tropical South America is 12 inches long, one of the largest of the 306 species of thrushes in the world. Thrushes in the tropics do not migrate. Various robins and nightingale-thrushes are year-round residents as far south as Peru and Bolivia.

100

Black-headed Sibia

The thrushes of Europe have given their British names to many American birds. The American robin was named for the British robin, which is only half as big. The EURASIAN REDSTART is a thrush. Its American namesake is a warbler. The EURASIAN BLACKBIRD is a thrush; the American blackbirds are a different family, the icterids. Common in Eurasian gardens are the SONG THRUSH and MISTLE THRUSH. In the field and brush and on the moors, common thrushes are the WHEATEAR, the NIGHTINGALE, and the FIELDFARE.

One of the most beautiful and tuneful of the Asian thrushes is the WHITE-RUMPED SHAMA of India. This is a popular cage bird in Asia and Europe. Almost as colorful is the WHITE-STARRED BUSH-ROBIN that is found on the slopes of Mt. Kilimanjaro and in other parts of Africa. Another bright thrush is the BLUETHROAT that flies to northern Africa for the winter after breeding in Sweden, Lapland, and northern Russia.

Varied Thrush
♂

American Redstart
♂

Thrushes feed on the ground where they move about as robins do with a sort of hop, skip, and jump. They do not catch insects in flight. They pick up bugs, beetles, worms, and often ants and snails from plants and the ground. They also pick small fruits wherever they grow.

101

Wheatear

Eurasian Blackbird ♂

Bluebird ♂

During migration and on the wintering grounds many thrushes travel and feed in flocks. In Florida a flock of robins will clean every berry from a 30-foot holly tree in a morning and look for another in the afternoon.

Thrushes build open cup-nests of plant material and trash cemented together with mud. They place their nests anywhere from ground level to the tops of high trees. American robins' nests have been found at every height and often in shrubbery close to houses. A few thrushes, like the bluebirds, place their nests in tree holes or bird boxes. The Eurasian ROCK THRUSHES and the WHEAT-EAR place their nests in crevices in rocks. The COMMON ROCK THRUSH sometimes nests in the ruins of stone castles and forts.

Male and female bluebirds work together to gather material, build a nest, and incubate the 4 to 6 pale blue eggs.

The male birds of the other thrushes do nothing to help their mates until the eggs hatch. Then they assist in feeding the young. When thrushes raise 2 or 3 families a year they usually build a new nest for each family. The chicks of the first brood of the EASTERN BLUEBIRD often help the parents feed the second brood. Thrushes' nests remain clean while the nestlings are in them. The droppings of the young birds are in little sacs which the parents carry away.

See also: ROBINS

Giant Tinamou

Little Tinamou

Tinamous

These are 45 species of forest and grassland birds that live the year round in Central and South America from Mexico to Argentina. They range in size from that of a plump domestic pigeon to a plump domestic hen. They live, nest, and feed on the ground, but they can fly. When in danger, they take to the air with a roar of wings and drop to the ground in the nearest underbrush that will hide them. Their flutelike voices can be heard in the jungle when the bird cannot be seen.

Panamanians call the GIANT TINAMOU *perdiz de arca*. Translated into English this is "partridge of the ark." The legend in Panama is that when the rainbow appeared over Noah's Ark its bright colors scared the giant tinamou so that the pair left the Ark and hid in the forest where they still hide. The eggs of tinamous reflect several colors of the rainbow. They are green or blue or yellow or purplish brown and shine in the light.

Tinamous raise from 1 to 10 chicks each year. The eggs are incubated by the male and he cares for the chicks. A day or two after the young hatch, he leads them to fruit, seeds, and insects, where they can feed themselves. Tinamous are game birds and delicious to eat. The meat is pale green but turns white when cooked.

103

Tufted Titmouse

Titmice

These trusting, friendly, teachable birds live in forests and brush lands. Their name comes from two Anglo-Saxon words "tit" and "mase" meaning small bird. And they are small—most of the 65 kinds, including the 7 American chickadees, are only 4 to 4½ inches long. The SULTAN TIT of eastern Asia, nearly 8 inches long, is the largest, and a giant among titmice. It is also the only really bright one, with a gleaming yellow crest and yellow breast. Most titmice are grayish or brownish birds with markings of black and white. The BLACK TIT of Africa is a bluish-black bird with only a little white on its wings.

The largest titmouse in America is the 5½-inch TUFTED TITMOUSE of the eastern United States. The GREAT TIT of Eurasia, the largest of the family in Europe, is the same size. The smallest titmouse is the PYGMY TIT of Java. Like the 3½-inch COMMON BUSH TIT of the western United States and Mexico, half of its 3 inches is tail.

Titmice spend most of their days busily searching for insects and insect eggs on trees and bushes. They eat small wild fruits and hang upside down to eat the seeds of spruce, hemlock, and pine. Most titmice do not really migrate, but wander in the same area the year round. They come to feeding stations, especially in winter, for seeds, suet and bits of apple. The tufted titmouse and the BLACK-CAPPED, CAROLINA, and BOREAL CHICKADEES in America become so tame that they will take food from the hand.

Titmice also eat nuts and acorns. Holding an acorn down with its foot, a titmouse hits the shell with its strong

Great Tit
♂

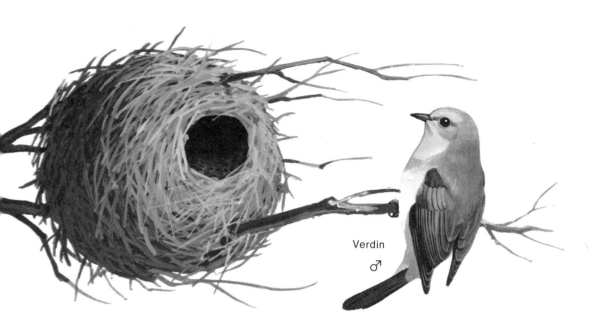

Verdin
♂

little cone-shaped bill until the acorn cracks. During the summer titmice hide nuts, acorns, and seeds for the winter. They are also clever at finding grass and weed seeds above snow-covered fields.

Most titmice build nests in holes in trees, fence posts, and rotting stubs, old woodpecker holes, rock cavities, or bird boxes. Black-capped chickadee pairs work together to chip out their own holes with their bills in half-rotten wood. The females usually build the nest. The material—grasses, feathers, hair, moss, plant down, and mammal fur— is sometimes brought by the male birds. The tufted titmouse and the Mexican border's BLACK-CRESTED TITMOUSE often use a discarded snake skin in their nests. Pairs of mated titmice raise broods of as many as 14 chicks. In America they usually raise from 7 to 10. Titmice often

feed their young on caterpillars. In England the great tit's chicks hatch just when leaf-eating caterpillars are most plentiful.

Titmice twitter and chirp. The chickadees have call notes that more or less sound like their name. The WILLOW TIT of Eurasia has a pleasant warbling song. Many titmouse songs are thin and high.

In Japan the VARIED TIT is a favorite cage bird and is kept in a special tall cage where it can exercise by turning its natural backward somersaults. It can be taught many tricks and is a common street performer.

Our American tufted titmouse has just a single trick. When it can't find hair elsewhere to build its nest, it may pull it out of a human head.

See also: CHICKADEES

Varied Tit
♂

Toucans

The huge bill of a toucan looks as though it were too heavy for the bird to carry. Because it is hollow, it weighs very little. It is strong because, like the wing of an airplane, it has supports inside it. The supports are made of a bony material with many cells like a honeycomb. Inside its mouth a toucan has a long slender flat tongue with notched edges and a bristly tip. In sunlight a toucan's bill glows like a stained-glass window.

Toucans use their huge bills to pick fruit. In prickly places they can do so without getting their faces into the thorns. Toucans take fruit, other birds' eggs and chicks, and water into the tips of their bills. Then they throw their heads back so food and drink fall into their throats. They also eat all sorts of insects. Probably their notched and bristly tongues help in insect catching.

The 37 kinds of toucans live in the forests of tropical America from southern Mexico south to southern Brazil. They follow each other when they fly weakly from tree to tree as though playing follow the leader. They seem to frighten enemies with their beaks but do not use them as weapons. When sleeping, toucans lay their bright bills along their backs and cover them with their upturned tails.

Toucans nest in hollow trees and stumps and also in the old holes left by their close relatives, the woodpeckers. The 2 to 4 white eggs hatch into naked chicks that do not look like their parents. Their beaks are broad and flat and the lower bill is slightly larger than the upper. For several months while their beaks and feathers grow, they sit on a growing pile of fruit pits that they and their parents spit out.

One of the smallest toucans is the 11-inch BLUE-THROATED TOUCANET of the mountains of Costa Rica and Panama. One of the largest toucans, over 20 inches long, is SWAINSON'S TOUCAN of northern South America north to Honduras. Toucans grunt but have no song.

Swainson's Toucan

Blue-throated Toucanet

Quetzal ♂

Gartered Trogon ♂

Towhees

See Sparrows and Related Birds

Trogons

Trogons are fruit-eating birds of the tropics of America, Asia, and Africa. They are famous for their brilliant metallic plumage. In the sun they glitter like hummingbirds. All 34 species of these 9- to 13-inch birds have bright pink, red, orange, or yellow bellies. All but a few have vivid green backs and tails.

The best known of the trogons is the QUETZAL of Central America. The male of this 14-inch bird wears a splendid train of 4 fernlike feathers that flow over his 7-inch tail. Quetzal nest in holes in rotten trees from 14 to 60 feet above the ground. They raise 2 broods of 2 to 4 chicks each spring. The female is a plainer green bird without a train and fits into the nest-hole. When the male incubates the eggs, his train bends over his head and hangs out of the hole. It looks more like an air plant growing on the tree than bird feathers.

The COPPERY-TAILED TROGON occasionally wanders into Arizona and Texas from Mexico. Like all the trogons except the quetzal it has a square tail and no train. It hovers in front of fruit while picking it off a tree with its bill.

107

Turkeys

Columbus discovered America in 1492, but he did not discover the turkey until 1502, when he visited Honduras on his fourth voyage. When he landed, the Indians brought the explorer a gift of food which included turkeys. These were probably domestic birds. Hundreds of years before Europeans found the New World, the Indians of Mexico had large flocks of tame turkeys.

In 1511, King Ferdinand of Spain ordered his ships to bring 10 tame turkeys, 5 male and 5 female, on every return voyage from America. From Spain they spread all over Europe. By 1577 large flocks of turkeys were common in English farmyards.

Strangely enough the ancestors of the domestic turkeys we eat today came from England. They were sent to the colony in Jamestown, Virginia, as soon as it was settled. The Pilgrim colony in Massachusetts received a shipment of tame turkeys in 1629.

The domestic turkey, like its ancestor the MEXICAN WILD TURKEY, has white tips on its tail feathers. No other turkey has the tail rimmed with white.

Before 1900, wild turkeys had disappeared from much of their range. Protective laws and new methods of raising wild birds have now restored turkeys to parts of their old range and introduced them to states where they were not native, such as California. In 1959 scientists estimated 453,249 wild turkeys in the United States.

Wild turkeys eat nuts, acorns, fruit, and insects. The nuts and acorns are swallowed whole and crushed between the pebbles in the turkey's gizzard. Most birds swallow pebbles and stones. These remain in their gizzards to grind food, the toothless birds' way of chewing. Turkeys stay near water so they can drink at least twice a day.

The show-off wild turkey gobbler mates with a number of hens. In early spring he seeks a tree with a broad horizontal branch. This will be his home for the season. He will fight to the death any other cock turkey who dares to come near it or his hens. During the night he roosts in his tree. During the day he

spreads his tail, swells the wattles on his chin, droops his wings until they drag, and struts back and forth on the branch. His loud gobbling brings his hens to him one at a time. When he sees a hen approach he jumps to the ground and continues his strutting courtship while she walks around him.

Hen turkeys build well-hidden nests, sometimes alone, sometimes 2 or 3 hens together. In the nest, each hen lays from 5 to 18 eggs. The hen or hens incubate the eggs for 28 days. As soon as the chicks hatch, the hen leads them away to hide because the cock is so jealous he will kill his own chicks.

The OCELLATED TURKEY that lives on the lowlands of the Yucatan, Guatemala, and British Honduras and the common turkey were used by the Indians for many things besides food. The bones were made into flutes, beads, bird callers, and a pointed tool for making holes in leather and wood called an awl. The feathers were made into feather cloth, quilts, capes, dresses, fans, and headdresses. The spurs on turkeys' legs were made into arrowheads for hunting small game. American settlers made pillows and mattresses of the feathers and brooms of the wings and fans of the tails. The French in Louisiana made umbrellas by fastening 4 turkey tails together.

Vireos

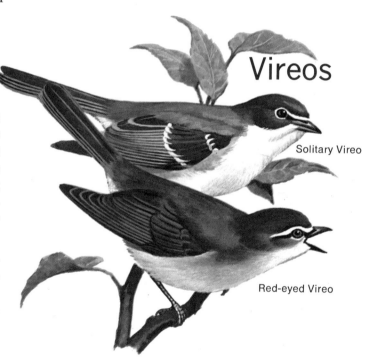

Solitary Vireo

Red-eyed Vireo

Vireos are grayish or olive brownish plain-feathered perching birds of the Americas. They are from 4 to 7 inches in length. The brightest of them have yellow breasts or throats. Those that breed in the Northern Hemisphere migrate to Central or South America or the West Indies in winter.

These insect-eaters hang their small cup- or cone-shaped nests in the V of a forked branch. The nests are so well hidden by leaves that the male birds often sing their sweet, warbling songs while incubating 3 to 5 eggs. BELL'S VIREO of California and the Midwest decorates its nest with flowers and the colored silk of cocoons. The WARBLING VIREO known from southern Canada to northern South America sings as many as 4,000 songs a day during the breeding season. He and his mate build a woven grass nest lined with feathers, hair, spider webs and sometimes bits of wool yarn.

The RED-EYED VIREO breeds across southern Canada and the United States except in the desert states. It winters in South America through Brazil. It is called "the preacher" because of its long monotonous song.

The PHILADELPHIA VIREO was named because it was first found near the city of Philadelphia, but it is only seen in Pennsylvania on migration. It breeds in Canada and northern New Hampshire, Michigan and North Dakota, and winters in Central America.

The SOLITARY VIREO is common in the temperate parts of North America. It winters in our southern states and Mexico.

109

Voice

The sounds birds make are an important part of their lives. The first sound made by a bird is the call for food of a newly hatched chick. One of the first sounds it recognizes is the call of its parents. It learns the calls that mean danger and, when it leaves the nest, the calls that mean "Here is food." In flight it learns the call that says "Stay with the flock" and the call that says "You can't feed in this place. You can't perch in this tree. This is my territory."

A bird uses its voice to attract a mate and to announce that it has found and held a nesting place. Among the perching birds, this is done by the songs of the males. Most of the 5,150 perching birds sing, but most of the remaining 3,405 species of birds in the world do not. They give various calls. They whistle, scream, caw, peep, hoot, trumpet, cackle, crow, or grunt.

The songs and calls of birds come from a voice box. The human voice box, the larynx, is in the throat, close to the mouth, at the top of the windpipe. A bird's voice box, the syrinx, is at the bottom of its windpipe close to its lungs. Air passing to and from the lungs, through the syrinx, flutters thin tissues. These create the sound which comes out through the mouth. Usually the more muscles a bird's syrinx has, the more notes the bird can sing. Birds like sparrows, thrushes, and the mockingbird family have syrinxes with a number of muscles and sing fine melodies.

The American vultures, the storks, ibises, and some pelicans have no syrinx at all and no voice. All they can do is push air out of their bills in hisses. Some ratites have no syrinx, but an air pouch is connected to the windpipes of the males. During the breeding season the air pouch can be blown up like a balloon, and from it comes a booming roar.

Each species of songbird has a distinctive song that identifies it. An individual song sparrow may have as many as 20 different ways of singing its song, but it always remains a song sparrow melody. It would never be mistaken for that of a white-throated sparrow or a swamp sparrow or the song of any other species of bird.

The calls of the birds may be similar in a family. Owls hoot, but no one would confuse the trembling, sad call of the screech owl with the 4 hoots, repeated in a lower tone, of the barred owl or the cuckoolike hoots of the burrowing owl. In the same way all pigeons and doves have soft, cooing notes, but no two are exactly alike.

Many birds like the spotted bowerbird, the mockingbird, and the superb lyrebird are mimics and imitate other birds. No one knows the reason for mimicry. Birds that learn to talk in captivity like parrots and the hill myna, a starling, are not mimics in the wild.

The songs and calls of many birds have been recorded on records and on tape. By listening to these recordings you can learn how to recognize the birds by their songs. Some sounds birds make are so high the human ear cannot hear them. We know these sounds are made because machines translate them into lines called sound spectrographs. This is a spectrograph of a song sparrow's song.

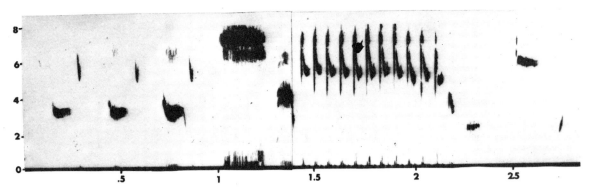

frequency in kilocycles

duration in seconds

Andean Condor

King Vulture

Turkey Vulture

Vultures

These 7 species of New World birds are meat-eaters. Deer that die in the forest, cattle and sheep that drop on the range, the animals killed by cars on the highways, and dead fish washed ashore are all vulture food. Vultures help to keep the Americas clean. If they did not eat as they do, governments and private people would spend millions of dollars every year to remove and bury or burn carrion.

With eyes that see about 8 times more sharply than man's, vultures soar far above the countryside watching the ground and each other. When a vulture sees carrion, it goes into a food flight and circles down. Other vultures see and follow from miles around. Vultures can grunt, but are almost voiceless so they cannot call to one another.

The talons and beaks of all vultures are too weak to lift or carry or tear anything strong. They must wait until the leathery hide of large animals rots before they can eat. Their heads look bare from a distance, but, from close up, they appear to have had crew cuts. These birds walk, perch, and stand firmly and with dignity, but when they try to run with half-open wings they lurch along lopsidedly.

Vultures raise 1 to 3 chicks once a year, or once every other year, depending on the species. They build no nests and lay their eggs on the bare ground, or in tree hollows, caves, or empty buildings. The TURKEY VULTURE that breeds from southern Canada to southern South America and the BLACK VULTURE that breeds from southern United States to southern South America both incubate their 2 eggs for 6 weeks. The young of all vultures hatch covered with down, including their heads, and do not leave the nesting place or fly until they are 3 months old or more. The turkey vulture chicks wear white and the black vulture chicks wear tan down.

Parent vultures carry food to their

111

chicks by swallowing it. At the nest, they gulp the half-digested meal back into their mouths. The chicks reach in and help themselves. Vultures, especially while breeding, eat the newly hatched young of herons and other birds and newborn mammals.

The KING VULTURE of Central and South America does not breed until it is 3 or 4 years old. At that time its head turns purple, green, and yellow. The YELLOW-HEADED VULTURE of the same area is very like our turkey vulture. It is particularly fond of dead lizards and has been seen carrying one in its weak bill, probably in order to eat it without sharing with companions.

The 40 CALIFORNIA CONDORS that still survived in 1966 and the ANDEAN CONDOR of the mountains of South America are the largest living vultures. California condors are 4 feet long and they have a wing span of 10 feet. The Andean condor sometimes feeds on newborn fawns and other helpless mammals. Condors incubate their eggs for 2 months. Condor chicks do not leave their cliff-side caves until they are about 5 months old.

The birds spoken of as vultures in the Old World are carrion-eating hawks. The GRIFFON VULTURE and the BEARDED VULTURE mentioned in the list of unclean birds in the Bible are among them.

Wagtails

See Pipits

Warblers

The Americas have no other birds that are so badly named as the warblers. Not one of the 119 kinds can warble. The sounds that come from warblers' throats are tseeps, tweets, twits, peets, tsips, tchips, chis, churs and zees.

None of these sounds could be considered "singing softly, in a trilling manner," which is what warbling means. It must have been their behavior that reminded John James Audubon of another family of very different Old World warblers that really warble in England. We should speak of our New World family as wood-warblers because they are birds of the woodlands.

Fifty-five species of wood-warblers breed in North America. Most of them winter in tropical Central and South America, where the other 64 species live the year round. Warblers are insect-eaters and must leave the north before cold kills the insects. A number of warblers breed in Canada and are seen in the United States only when migrating. Most male warblers are easy to recognize in spring when they wear bright breeding plumage. In fall the males are almost as dully dressed as the females, and all the young birds are, too. It is then hard to tell one species from another.

Most warblers are around 4 or 5 inches long but one giant, the YELLOW-BREASTED CHAT, measures $7\frac{1}{4}$ inches. This strange warbler mimics other birds with its strong, squeaky voice. It breeds throughout the United States and northern Mexico, and winters in Central America. The commonest North American warbler is the MYRTLE WARBLER, which breeds north of the Great Lakes, and winters south through Central America. It eats bayberries and poison ivy berries in cold weather. The YELLOW-THROAT that breeds from central Canada to southern Mexico says "witchity, witchity." The yellow-throats that live in the south do not migrate but those that live in the north leave in winter.

Less than a thousand KIRTLAND'S WAR-

BLERS nest in jack pine trees in central Michigan and nowhere else. They winter in the Bahama Islands.

Most warblers build cup-shaped nests on the ground, in bushes, in trees, or in holes in trees or banks. A few, such as the OVENBIRD of eastern North America, build covered nests near or on the ground with a side entrance like the brick oven of colonial days. Nest-building is usually done by the females and they alone incubate the 4 to 5 brown-speckled white eggs. Often, during the 11 to 14 days the female sits on the nest, the male feeds her. He helps to feed the naked or nearly naked chicks that remain in the nest for another 8 to 14 days.

Many cowbirds lay eggs in warblers' nests. Then the adult warblers work very hard searching bark and leaves to find insects to feed the foster chick.

Most North American warblers are greenish, yellowish, or bluish-gray birds. But the AMERICAN REDSTART, which breeds in Canada and the northeastern United States, is a white-breasted black bird with bold orange markings. The 4-inch YELLOW WARBLER that breeds through most of North America is a bright flash in suburban gardens and orchards, and the noisy yellow-breasted chat has a breast brighter than any daffodil.

The North American warblers migrate at night. When bad weather blinds them they fly into skyscrapers, monuments, lighthouses, and television towers. Thousands of night migrants are killed this way, and more warblers than any other family of birds are among the dead picked up after a night of poor visibility. Migrating warblers are also killed when giant searchlights at airports blind them so they fly into the light and collide with each other.

Myrtle Warbler

Yellow-breasted Chat

Canada Goose

Nene

Black Swan

Mute Swan

Waterfowl

This gathering of ducks, geese, and swans are called wildfowl in England. They are also known as the duck family. Geese and swans are really just big ducks. The 145 species range through waters in and around the lands of the world from the Arctic southward except Antarctica.

Waterfowl all have rather short legs set well back on their chunky bodies, webbed front toes, and flat "duck bills." The bills of most have strainer edges, so mud and sand is sifted out of the birds' mouths, leaving small animals, worms, weed seeds, and grain, roots, and greens to be swallowed. Waterfowl swim well using their feet as paddles, and most of them dive either for food or to escape enemies. The northernmost species fly well and migrate long distances to southern wintering grounds. Some fly well but do not migrate, and four species are flightless. On migration and on food flights they often fly in a V-formation. Waterfowl travel, feed, and rest in groups. Many species nest in colonies close together and others in loose groups, each pair within sight of another.

Although most waterfowl stay mated for life, courtship is repeated each spring. Male and female swim toward each other dipping their heads down into the water as though bowing. All geese, all swans, and most ducks build their nests on the ground. The nests are bulky piles of grasses, roots, sticks, and odds and ends. Most of them are lined with down feathers which the female plucks from her own breast. A few ducks build on rock ledges or stumps, or in holes in the ground, or in trees, or in bird boxes. Waterfowl lay from 3 to 18 eggs. They are incubated, mostly by the females, for 21 days among the smaller ducks and up to 43 days among the swans. The downy young hatch within a few hours of one another, and are soon ready to follow the female into the water.

The duck takes care of her ducklings without any help from her mate, the drake. The "pen" swan and her mate, the "cob," take care of the "cygnets" together until they are on the wing. The goose and her mate, the gander, remain with their goslings in a family group

Mandarin Duck ♂

Wood Ducks ♀ ♂

until the next nesting season.

Adult waterfowl molt during the breeding season. Females molt while they are grounded taking care of their chicks, and males on their feeding grounds. They lose all their wing and tail flight feathers at once. Flightless like the chicks, they escape enemies by diving and hiding. By the time the chicks take wing, the adults have grown new flight feathers. They all leave the nesting grounds together.

The largest and most graceful of the waterfowl are the 7 swans: 5 white swans of the Northern Hemisphere, the BLACK-NECKED SWAN of southern South America and the BLACK SWAN of Australia. Swans grow necks that are longer than their bodies and hold their necks in lovely curves. They move on the surface of the water as smoothly and as gracefully as sailboats carried along by a light wind. On land swans tend to walk heavily with a waddle, but their size gives them dignity.

Some swans reach a length of 5 feet and weigh up to 50 pounds. The largest

is the TRUMPETER SWAN of North America. The commonest swan in North America, the WHISTLING SWAN, nests at the edge of the Arctic Circle and winters southward into the United States.

The MUTE SWAN, a native of Eurasia, is not really mute. It makes various grunting, hissing noises. It has been carried all over the world to decorate lakes in parks and gardens. It is a bird of beauty, but not a good pet as it is often bad tempered. When mute swan chicks first fly any distance, they often do so above a flying parent. When they tire, they drop onto the parent bird's back for a ride.

The tribe of 14 geese are smaller than the swans but still big birds. The CANADA GOOSE, familiar all over North America except on the Florida Peninsula, and the GRAY-LAG GOOSE of northern Europe are the largest. They are as long as 3 feet and weigh up to 18 pounds.

For a long time, everyone thought that the LESSER SNOW GOOSE and the BLUE GOOSE, which breed at the edge of the Arctic and winter in the United

Blue-winged Teal ♂

Shoveler ♂

Mallard ♂

Green-winged Teal ♂

Pintail ♂

States, were different species. In 1929 the unknown breeding ground of the blue goose was discovered on Baffin Island. Lo and behold! A blue goose's eggs sometimes hatch lesser snow geese and a lesser snow goose's eggs sometimes hatch blue geese. So they are one species with two colors of feathers. Now they are both called blue geese.

The WHITE-FRONTED GOOSE breeds at the edge of the Arctic in Siberia and western North America and winters southward. Its high pleasant honk has given it the name "laughing goose." The BEAN GOOSE of Eurasia was so called, because it arrived on its wintering grounds just in time to eat the waste beans left in the bean fields. All geese graze in fields and meadows like cattle. They often eat waste grain. The strange MAGPIE GOOSE of Australia and New Guinea, which has a knob on its head, often perches on trees. Like the NENE of Hawaii, it does not migrate.

The nene originally lived on the dry mountains of Hawaii in summer, getting what water it needed by eating juicy plants. In winter it moved down to lower ground where it raised its 2 to 4 young. Unlike other geese it has very little webbing between its toes. It rarely goes near the water in the wild, but it enjoys swimming in captivity.

After settlers arrived in Hawaii, the nene was almost wiped out. The birds were shot and their nests and eggs destroyed by the pigs, rats and mongooses that the settlers brought with them. Now, nearly 300 live wild in two sanctuaries established by the federal government.

Among the 124 kinds of ducks, the ones most likely to be seen in the United States are members of the large tribe of dipping ducks and the tribe of bay ducks. The dipping ducks are those that feed by tipping into the water without diving. In this group, male and female wear different plumage. The MALLARD, the most easily tamed of the wild ducks, is a dipping duck. It is found in the Northern Hemisphere around the world. Other dipping ducks are the BLACK DUCK, loved by

Lesser Scaup ♂

Bufflehead ♂

Canvasback ♂

Oldsquaw ♂

♂ King Eider

sportsmen in eastern North America, the widely known PINTAIL, the BLUE-WINGED, the GREEN-WINGED, the CINNAMON TEAL, and the SHOVELER.

The AUKLAND ISLAND TEAL from islands near New Zealand has lost the power to fly but swims around its island.

The many-colored BAIKAL TEAL is a dipping duck from Asia as is the MANDARIN DUCK, so like our WOOD DUCK. The last 2 breed in holes in trees, and will use a bird box shaped like a small barrel laid on its side. Mandarin ducks and wood ducks mate for life. The pair swim and fly side by side the year round.

Bay ducks dive from the surface and swim under water to feed, eating many small animals. They are heavy birds that must run along the water with flapping wings before they can take off into the air. Most of these low-quacking ducks breed inland. They migrate overland and winter along the coasts. In America, the CANVASBACK, the REDHEAD, the RING-NECKED DUCK and the GREATER and LESSER SCAUP do their breeding in the north

and winter southward. The BUFFLEHEAD and COMMON GOLDENEYE winter in inland waters across the United States as well as on the coasts. The common goldeneye does the same thing in Eurasia. A number of Eurasian bay ducks are called pochards.

Most of the deep diving "sea ducks" breed on northern islands and winter off the coasts. They include the eiders, the scoters and the yodeling, whistling OLDSQUAW that breeds in the Arctic the world around. The oldsquaw winters on the Great Lakes and the St. Lawrence River as well as the seacoasts in North America. It is known as the LONG-TAILED DUCK in England. The COMMON, the KING, the SPECTACLED, and STELLER'S EIDERS all breed in arctic lands. They are valuable to the northern people who harvest the down lining of their nests to make quilts and winter clothing. When the nest is relined the birds are not disturbed, so they return year after year each to the same place.

See also: DOMESTIC BIRDS

117

Weaverbirds

Although this is one of the largest families of birds in the world, its natural range is limited to Eurasia and Africa. Among the weaverbirds are birds called sparrows, widowbirds, and queleas, as well as weavers.

The 6-inch HOUSE SPARROW, often spoken of as the ENGLISH SPARROW, has with the help of man spread to every place where seed-eating birds can live except a few ocean islands. Homesick Englishmen introduced them wherever they settled. Adaptable and pushy, house sparrows quickly made a place for themselves. As each pair raises 2 broods of at least 5 or 6 young a year, their numbers increase by leaps and bounds. In the United States a few hundred pairs of house sparrows were released in a Brooklyn, New York, cemetery in 1852. Today millions of house sparrows are dooryard birds throughout North America.

House sparrows are not the only weaverbirds in America. EUROPEAN TREE SPARROWS of Eurasia were imported from Germany in 1870 and released in a St. Louis park. They are not pushy birds, but they increased and now breed in Missouri and southwestern Illinois. Male and female European tree sparrows wear the same plumage and share the work of incubation and care of their 4 to 6 young early each spring. In Japan these same sparrows are netted in the wild and sold to housewives who broil them.

Weaverbirds have earned their name by weaving complicated nests. The SOCIAL WEAVERS of southern Africa build the most complex nests of any birds in the world. Social weavers look very much like house sparrows and are only 5½ inches long. Yet they build a nest that has often been mistaken at a distance for a native hut. From 20 to 50 mated pairs of social weavers band together to weave a waterproof roof of straw. It may be 15 feet across and cover a 10-foot-high bird apartment house. Each pair builds its own apartment, hanging it from the roof. Each has a separate en-

Long-tailed Widowbird ♂

European Tree Sparrow ♂

House Sparrow ♂

Cardinal Quelea ♂

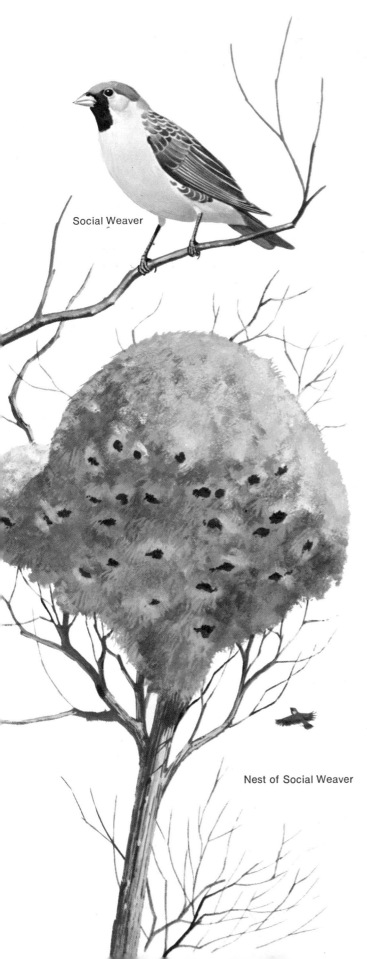

Social Weaver

Nest of Social Weaver

trance passage, up which the pair fly to tend their 2 to 4 chicks and feed them on grass seeds and insects.

The BAYA WEAVERBIRD of India is a trained street entertainer. At its master's word it picks up with its bill whatever color bead a customer asks for. It can also recognize numbers from 1 to 5. It earns its master's living.

The males of most species of weaverbirds wear brighter feathers than the females during the breeding season. The male LONG-TAILED WIDOWBIRD of southeast Africa is usually about 4 inches long. But during the breeding season, he grows a 9-inch drooping tail which he can spread like a fan in dry weather. In wet weather the tail sometimes becomes so heavy with water that he cannot fly and so can be caught by hand. He takes 6 to 10 mates who wear drab greenish-gray plumage. These females each build a thick-walled, ball-shaped nest with a side entrance near or on the ground. Each female lays 3 or 4 greenish-white eggs, about three fourths of an inch long, in her own nest.

Queleas are weaverbirds that travel in enormous flocks in grass country or cultivated fields when they are not breeding. They eat every seed and every kernel of corn as they go. The CARDINAL QUELEA of south Central Africa works a day and a half with his mate to weave a dome-shaped nest of fine grass with a side entrance. They hang it close to the ground from plant stems and pull a leaf over it to form a roof. Cardinal quelea's 2 or 3 eggs may be pale pink, blue, or green, spotted with brown and purple. The male bird wears a crimson hood during the breeding season, which depends on when the rainy season ripens the seeds they need to feed their chicks.

All weaverbirds are noisy and are constantly calling, chirping, and twitting, but none has a true song or melody.

Whip-poor-wills

See Nightjars

Woodcocks

See Snipes

Woodpeckers

Yellow-shafted Flicker ♂

Pileated Woodpecker

Yellow-bellied Sapsucker

In the Americas, Eurasia, and Africa where big trees grow, woodpeckers advertise themselves the year round by their harsh calls and also by the rat-a-tat of their bills hitting wood. They use their strong slender necks and heads as hammers and their bills as chisels to carve roosting holes and nesting holes in trees and banks. They also bore into wood or soil for food. They even signal to each other by drumming.

Woodpeckers have unusually long sticky, hairy tongues, with rakelike barbs on the tip. The woodpecker can reach with its tongue into the hole it has drilled and rake out the grubs and larvae. Small insects are caught in the sticky hairs. Most American woodpeckers feed this way, but the YELLOW-SHAFTED FLICKER, the RED-SHAFTED FLICKER and the GILDED FLICKER usually feed on the ground. They bore in the dirt for ants and other insects. The gilded flicker lives in the western deserts and digs its nest-holes in giant saguaro cactus trees. The YELLOW-BELLIED SAPSUCKER, one of the few migrating woodpeckers, feeds by drilling holes in trees and drinking the sap that runs out. It sometimes eats fruit as well. The yellow-bellied sapsucker is known across the continent from central Canada through Central America and in the West Indies.

The most widely spread and common North American woodpeckers are the look-alike HAIRY WOODPECKER and the DOWNY WOODPECKER. Both live year round from coast to coast from Alaska to Florida but the hairy woodpecker is also found south to Panama and in the Bahamas. It stays in forests in the summer

♂

Hairy Woodpecker

on its stiff tail while it bores for insects. If once caught in a bird bander's trap, it does not enter again but reaches its long tongue and bill through the wire to nip up a tidbit of bread. Red-headed woodpeckers also catch flying insects.

All American woodpecker pairs live and nest far from one another except the ROCK FLICKER of the mountains of western South America which nests in groups. Like the GROUND WOODPECKER of South Africa, it drills nesting holes in hillsides and ledges, tunneling like a kingfisher. The ground woodpecker, like the American flickers, eats ground insects and ants.

When a pair of woodpeckers chisel out their nesting hole, chips of wood fall to the bottom of the hole. On this pile of chips the female lays her glossy, round, white eggs. Most woodpeckers usually lay 4 to 6 eggs. A few lay 2 or 3 eggs and flickers lay 6 to 8. Male and female take turns incubating the eggs for 11 to 14 days. They feed the young for 3 to 5 weeks, flying back and forth with mouthfuls of insects.

Around the world in the far north and in high mountains of the Northern Hemisphere lives the NORTHERN THREE-TOED WOODPECKER. In Canada and the Rocky Mountains of the United States lives the BLACK-BACKED THREE-TOED WOODPECKER. These 2 species puzzle scientists by hatching with one less toe than all the other 208 kinds of woodpeckers. Woodpeckers with 3 toes or 4 have no trouble perching any way they want to and climbing up and down telephone poles and trees. Even the minia-

but moves into tree-planted towns and villages in winter. The downy woodpecker is one of the few woodpeckers that nest in scattered trees, orchards, suburban gardens, and even city parks.

The ACORN WOODPECKER of the United States' West Coast and southwestern states ranges through Central America. It carves nest-holes in dead pine trees, near where oaks grow. It stores acorns for the time when food is scarce. It drills a separate hole for each acorn and leaves its storehouse tree looking like a peg-board.

The brilliant RED-HEADED WOODPECKER lives east of the Rockies in the United States. Those that breed near the Canadian border move southward in winter. The red-headed woodpecker feeds like other typical woodpeckers. It clings to tree trunks with its toes and props itself up

ture 4-inch woodpeckers of the tropics, called piculets, climb about nimbly.

The 4 largest woodpeckers in the world all have crests. They have been disappearing as the forests of the Americas have been cut down. The 19-inch-long IVORY-BILLED WOODPECKER, once of the southeastern United States and Cuba, may survive in Texas, but the last firm record was in Cuba in the 1940's.

The 22-inch IMPERIAL WOODPECKER of the Mexican highlands has retired to a few places where pine trees with trunks 30 inches thick still stand. They are disappearing, according to a 1962 study, because the few survivors are being shot. The 15½-inch-long MAGELLANIC WOODPECKER of southern South America, called the "great carpenter" by the natives, was spoken of in 1897 as very scarce. It is even scarcer today. These big three need trees higher than a 4-story building with trunks 24 or more inches thick in which to carve their large nest holes. Most such trees fell to the lumberman's ax long ago.

The fourth big woodpecker, the 16½-inch-long PILEATED WOODPECKER of North America is more adaptable than the other three. It is willing to nest near the ground if it cannot find a tall tree.

The pileated woodpecker looks much like the ivory-billed woodpecker but its bill is dark, not ivory-white, and it does not have any white markings on its back. The female ivory-billed woodpecker has a black crest, the male a red crest. Both male and female pileated woodpeckers wear red crests and their wings and backs are as black as a crow's.

Wrens

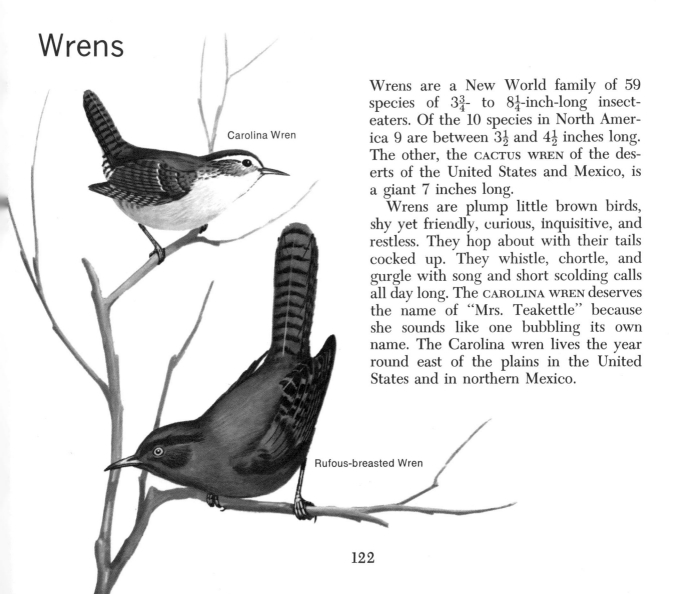

Carolina Wren

Rufous-breasted Wren

Wrens are a New World family of 59 species of $3\frac{3}{4}$- to $8\frac{1}{4}$-inch-long insect-eaters. Of the 10 species in North America 9 are between $3\frac{1}{2}$ and $4\frac{1}{2}$ inches long. The other, the CACTUS WREN of the deserts of the United States and Mexico, is a giant 7 inches long.

Wrens are plump little brown birds, shy yet friendly, curious, inquisitive, and restless. They hop about with their tails cocked up. They whistle, chortle, and gurgle with song and short scolding calls all day long. The CAROLINA WREN deserves the name of "Mrs. Teakettle" because she sounds like one bubbling its own name. The Carolina wren lives the year round east of the plains in the United States and in northern Mexico.

Wrens are busybodies. They poke their way into odd places to see what is going on. The commonest busybody wren in the Americas is the HOUSE WREN that pokes around in brush and shrubbery from central Canada to Tierra del Fuego.

The 49 Central and South American wrens include one of the world's finest singers, the QUADRILLE WREN. Male and female BUFF-BREASTED WRENS of Panama harmonize with one another in duets and the RUFOUS-BREASTED WREN is said to sing "Billy tea, boiling for me" loudly and clearly.

Thousands of years ago some of the WINTER WRENS that breed from Alaska to mid-California along the West Coast crossed into Asia. Now our winter wren breeds on the Aleutian Islands, the Kurile Islands, and Japan along its path into the warmer parts of Eurasia and northern Africa. It also nests in eastern North America along the Canadian border. It winters south to the Gulf of Mexico. Wrens that live in the tropics and sub-tropics do not migrate.

In spring a male wren returns to his nesting place and sings loudly to tell other male wrens to stay off his land and to tell a female he is ready to set up housekeeping. When a mate accepts him, he may help her build a nest. As soon as she lays her 4 to 10 cream or white eggs and starts to incubate them the male goes back to singing. If he is a North American wren, he may set up one or two other mates in other nests on his property.

The cactus wren builds a football-shaped nest with a covered side-porch entrance on top of cholla cactus or thorny bushes. The CANYON WREN of the mountain canyons of the western United States and Mexico and the ROCK WREN that ranges in the west from southern Canada through Central America both nest in rock crevasses and under ledges. The rock wren lays a pavement of bits of rock, shell, and bone on the floor of its nesting hole. The winter wren builds a moss- and twig-

covered nest with side entrance in up-rooted tree roots, under banks, or among fallen logs.

BEWICK'S WREN, known in many parts of the United States south of the Great Lakes and in Mexico, the house wren, and the Carolina wren are famous for nesting most anywhere they can find a roof over their heads. If no bird box or natural hole is found, they will make use of a flower pot, an empty tin can, a coat pocket, hat, basket, box, mailbox, watering can, or teapot without a lid. One pair of house wrens built its nest on the rear axle of an automobile. They went back and forth to work with the owner every day while 9 eggs were incubated for 13 days and until the chicks could fly.

The WRENTIT of western North America is the only one of the 282 members of the babbler family in the New World. Babblers are noisy, drab perching birds of Eurasia, Africa, Australia, and the Pacific Islands.

Wrens roost at night in empty nests and some use cavities in trees. Wrens bathe in dust as well as water and some bathe in morning dew.

Cactus Wren

About the Authors

Elizabeth S. Austin has been writing about birds since 1960. Her weekly nature column ran in a Florida newspaper for several years. She contributed the material on birds for the *Junior Encyclopedia of Natural History* and has written two Random House titles, *Penguins: The Birds With Flippers* and *Birds That Stopped Flying.* She edited the journals of the ornithologist Frank M. Chapman. Mrs. Austin was born in New York City and attended St. Elizabeth Academy in Convent, New Jersey. A Research Associate on the staff of the Florida State Museum, a department of the University of Florida, she lives with her husband, Dr. Oliver L. Austin, Jr., in Gainesville.

Oliver L. Austin, Jr., after graduating from Wesleyan University, earned his Ph.D. at Harvard. He is the author of *Birds of Newfoundland Labrador, Birds of Korea, Birds of Japan,* and *Birds of the World,* and also of many articles in scientific publications. He has done research in wildlife for the federal government, as Director of the Austin Ornithological Research Station on Cape Cod, as a member of General MacArthur's staff in Japan, and on the faculty of the Air War College in Alabama. At present Dr. Austin is Curator of Birds at the Florida State Museum and serves as editor of *Auk,* the journal of the American Ornithologists' Union, and of the Bulletin of the Florida State Museum.

About the Artist

Richard E. Amundsen has been a wildlife illustrator for the past six years. He contributes regularly to *Field and Stream.* His paintings have been shown throughout the country and hang in many private collections. Born and educated in California, Mr. Amundsen now lives in Seattle, Washington, with his wife, Lee, and their son and daughter.

Index